The Land and People of

CHINA

The Land and People of®

CHINA

by *John S. Major*

J. B. LIPPINCOTT   NEW YORK

Country maps by Susan M. Johnston/Melissa Turk & The Artist Network.

THE LAND AND PEOPLE OF
is a registered trademark of
Harper & Row, Publishers, Inc.

The Land and People of China
Copyright © 1989 by John S. Major
Printed in the U.S.A. All rights reserved.
For information address J. B. Lippincott Junior Books,
10 East 53rd Street, New York, N.Y. 10022.

Library of Congress Cataloging-in-Publication Data
Major, John S.
    The land and people of China / by John S. Major.
        p.   cm. — (Portraits of the nations series)
    Bibliography: p.
    Includes index.
    Summary: An introduction to the geography, history, culture,
economy, and government of China.
    ISBN 0-397-32336-0 : $ ISBN 0-397-32337-9 (lib. bdg.) : $
    1. China—Juvenile literature.   [1. China.]   I. Title.
II. Series.
DS706.M25 1989   88-23427
951—dc 19   CIP
                                                                AC

Typography by Harriett Barton
10 9 8 7 6 5 4 3 2 1
First Edition

For my father,
William P. Major
And in memory of my mother,
Kathryn Demarest Major

Contents

THE WORLD

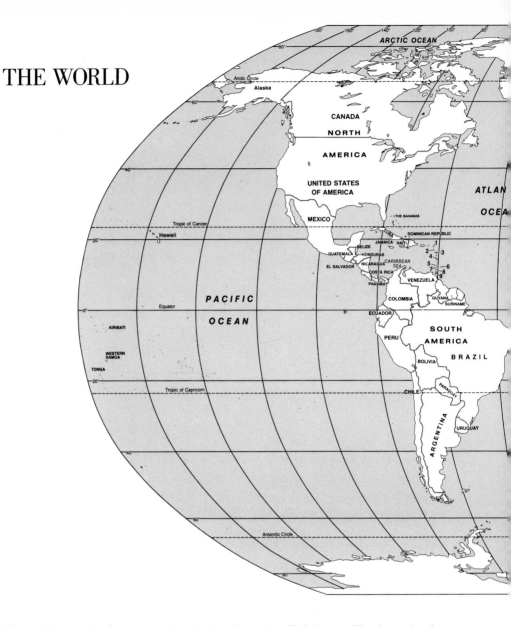

This world map is based on a projection developed by Arthur H. Robinson. The shape of each country and its size, relative to other countries, are more accurately expressed here than in previous maps. The map also gives equal importance to all of the continents, instead of placing North America at the center of the world. *Used by permission of the Foreign Policy Association.*

Legend

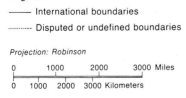

—— International boundaries

·········· Disputed or undefined boundaries

Projection: Robinson

Caribbean Nations

1. Anguilla
2. St. Christopher and Nevis
3. Antigua and Barbuda
4. Dominica
5. St. Lucia
6. Barbados
7. St. Vincent
8. Grenada
9. Trinidad and Tobago

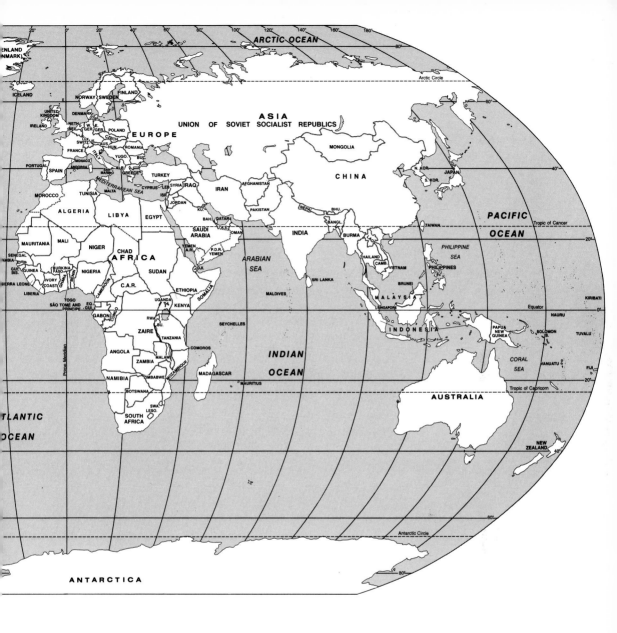

Abbreviations

ALB.	—Albania	C.A.R.	—Central African Republic	LEB.	—Lebanon	RWA.	—Rwanda
AUS.	—Austria	CZECH.	—Czechoslovakia	LESO.	—Lesotho	S. KOR.	—South Korea
BANGL.	—Bangladesh	DJI.	—Djibouti	LIE.	—Liechtenstein	SWA.	—Swaziland
BEL.	—Belgium	E.GER.	—East Germany	LUX.	—Luxemburg	SWITZ.	—Switzerland
BHU.	—Bhutan	EQ. GUI.	—Equatorial Guinea	NETH.	—Netherlands	U.A.E.	—United Arab Emirates
BU.	—Burundi	GUI. BIS.	—Guinea Bissau	N. KOR.	—North Korea	W. GER.	—West Germany
BUL.	—Bulgaria	HUN.	—Hungary	P.D.R.–YEMEN	—People's Democratic	YEMEN A.R.	—Yemen Arab Republic
CAMB.	—Cambodia	ISR.	—Israel		Republic of Yemen	YUGO.	—Yugoslavia

Mini Facts

OFFICIAL NAME: People's Republic of China. The Republic of China occupies Taiwan, claims all of China; not recognized officially by the United States.

LOCATION: East Asia south of Siberia and Mongolia, including Tibet and part of Central Asia. Common borders with North Korea in the northeast, the Soviet Union and the Mongolian People's Republic in the north, Afganistan, Pakistan, and India in the west and southwest, Nepal, Bhutan, India, Burma, Laos, and Vietnam in the south. Eastern boundary formed by the South China Sea, the East China Sea, the Yellow Sea, and the Bohai Gulf. Includes Taiwan and Hainan Islands; China also claims the Paracel and Spratley Islands in the South China Sea.

AREA: 3,719,275 square miles (9,632,922 square kilometers)

CAPITAL: Beijing

POPULATION: 1,065,138,000 (1986 est.)

MAJOR LANGUAGE: Chinese

RELIGIONS: Officially atheistic; Buddhism, Daoism, and various popular religions are practiced; there are small Islamic and Christian populations.

TYPE OF GOVERNMENT: Socialist Republic

HEAD OF STATE: President

HEAD OF GOVERNMENT: Premier

HEAD OF RULING PARTY: General Secretary

PARLIAMENT:. National People's Congress enacts laws; Communist Party Congress sets policy

ADULT LITERACY: 80% (1986 est.)

LIFE EXPECTANCY: Female, 69.4; Male, 65.5 (1985)

MAIN PRODUCTS: *Agriculture*—rice, wheat, corn, other grains; cotton, tobacco, oilseeds, sugarcane, tea, meat, fish, peanuts, sweet potatoes, fruit
Manufacturing and Processing—iron and steel, plastics, textiles (man-made fibers, cotton, silk), garments, trucks and tractors, rolling stock, ships, machine tools, electric and electronic equipment
Mining—Petroleum, natural gas, iron, coal, tungsten, antimony, manganese, mercury, phosphates, potash, tin

CURRENCY: Renminbi (also called Yuan)

A Note on the
Pronunciation of Chinese

The Chinese language is written in ideograms or "characters." Chinese characters are symbols of words, but they do not *spell* words; the pronunciation of each character must be learned independently of its written form. Many systems have been devised to use alphabetical writing to render the pronunciation of Chinese. No system is completely satisfactory. This book employs the *pinyin* system of spelling that is officially promoted by the People's Republic of China; although its spelling looks strange, it can give a reasonable approximation of the sound of spoken Chinese if its conventions are learned. (For the sake of simplicity, no attempt has been made here to indicate or reproduce the tonal values that are an integral part of Chinese pronunciation.)

Pinyin spelling uses five vowels: *a, e, i, o,* and *u*; they are normally pronounced "ah" as in c*a*r, "eh" as in l*e*t, "ee" as in *ee*l, "aw" as in l*a*w, and "oo" as in t*oo*l. *Every Chinese character is pronounced as a single* *syllable*; vowel combinations thus are pronounced as compound vowels. For example, *mao* is pronounced as in *mou*th, not as in *mayo*nnaise. *Yi* is pronounced long *e* as in *eel*, *iu* is pronounced as in *yo*del, *ou* is "oh" as in h*o*pe, and so on. And *i* as a *final* vowel following c, s, or z is pronounced "uh" as in h*uh*; following ch, sh, or zh it is pronounced "ur" as in *ur*gent.

Consonants are pronounced as they would be in English, with the following exceptions:

c as an initial sound is pronounced "ts." Thus *ci* is pronounced "tsuh."

q is pronounced as "ch." Thus *qin* is pronounced "chin"; *qu* is "cheu."

x is a softened "sh" sound, almost "sy." Thus *xin* is pronounced "syin."

z is pronounced as "dz." Thus *zou* is pronounced "dzoh."

zh is pronounced "j." Thus *zhou* is pronounced "joh."

The use of pinyin romanization makes some Chinese words that have been familiar in older forms look strange; *it does not change their pronunciation, however, but only the way they are spelled in English.* Thus "Peking" becomes "Beijing," "Taoism" becomes "Daoism," and Mao Tse-tung" becomes "Mao Zedong."

In two cases, older spellings have been retained here. First, two famous Chinese figures are widely known in the west by non-Mandarin dialect pronunciations of their names: Sun Yat-sen and Chiang Kai-shek. (In Mandarin pronunciation and pinyin romanization, they would be Sun Yixian and Jiang Jieshi.) Second, as a matter of courtesy, names of officials of the Republic of China on Taiwan are spelled in the older Wade-Giles system that remains in official use there; for example, Chiang Ching-kuo.

A young woman in Shanghai. Her contemporary clothing symbolizes China's recent drive for modernization.

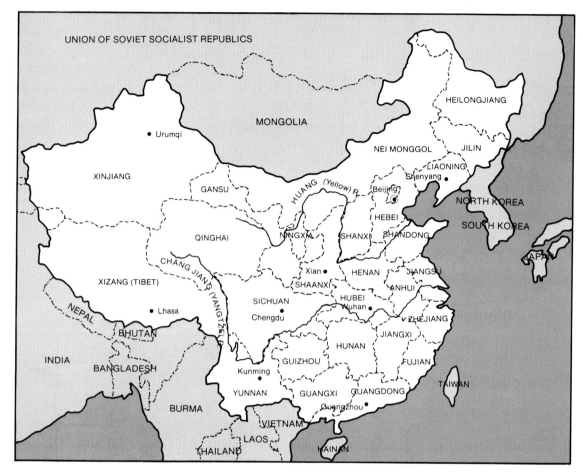

Political Map: China and Its Neighbors

Being Chinese

There are more than one billion Chinese people in the world today; one of every five people in the world is Chinese. But what does it mean to say that a person is Chinese? Are there any characteristics that can unite and give a common identity to such an enormous number of people? Is a Chinese person simply anyone who is a citizen of China? Do all citizens of China regard themselves as Chinese? How do we classify a Chinese-speaking citizen of Singapore, or a third-generation Chinese American in San Francisco's Chinatown?

The answers to these questions lie in the long history of the land and people of China. China is as much an idea as it is a place; and to be Chinese is to share in a particular cultural identity. Huge numbers of people, across many generations—and despite wide differences in language, geography, and life-style—have been able to say, "We are Chinese," thus defining themselves in a particular way.

The Middle Kingdom

One of the oldest expressions of Chinese self-identity is the word *Zhongguo*, which means "The Middle Kingdom." As large areas of northern China came under the control of a succession of unified kingdoms—a process that began around 4000 years ago—the people of those kingdoms thought of themselves as living in the center of the world. Their society was, for them, the only civilization worthy of the name. One was either a civilized person, living in the Middle Kingdom, or else a barbarian living on the periphery of the Middle Kingdom or in the howling wilderness beyond.

But the Middle Kingdom was not defined as a particular piece of territory. It had no definite boundaries. The early kings of China, and later the emperors as well, instead thought of their realm as being *tianxia*, "all under heaven." If the barbarians living beyond the center were not Chinese, it was not because they lived on the other side of a frontier. Rather, it was because they had not yet realized the benefits of becoming Chinese: accepting the ruler of the Middle Kingdom as their king, and adopting the norms of Chinese civilization as their own. In theory, the Middle Kingdom could expand—not infinitely, but enough to incorporate any territory in which it was possible to live a civilized life.

The Middle Kingdom did expand greatly. Over the course of centuries, even before the development (about 2000 years ago) of the forms of rule that we describe as an "empire," the area ruled by the Chinese kings grew. At first a small state on the North China Plain, it spread to include all of Northern and Central China, and portions of the coastal regions of Southern China. In the process, many groups of people who had once been thought of as "barbarians" became "Chinese."

The Role of Language

The Chinese concept of civilization is closely linked to the Chinese language. Speaking some form of Chinese, and even more, having access to the large and growing body of literature written in Chinese characters, became essential to the Chinese understanding of what it meant to be civilized. For most of Chinese history, most people in China were illiterate; but they were still Chinese. For them, also, writing was part of the definition of civilization. They lived in an environment in which literacy was at least potentially available to them, and accepted the general Chinese belief that a knowledge of reading and writing was the fundamental qualification for membership in the ruling class.

The Chinese language contains many different dialects. These are not simply regional accents; rather they are forms of spoken Chinese that have evolved to become completely mutually unintelligible. Particularly in southeastern China, spoken dialects are very different from standard northern Chinese (the language that many westerners call "Mandarin" —the language of the Beijing-based government officials—and that the Chinese themselves call "the national language" or "common speech"). Mandarin, Cantonese, and Fukienese are as different from one another as French, Italian, and Spanish. They share a great deal of vocabulary (but in quite different pronunciations), and a common grammatical structure, but a person who speaks only Cantonese cannot be understood by a person who knows only Mandarin. But, remarkably, all dialects of spoken Chinese can be written down in exactly the same way, and understood by everyone regardless of how the words are pronounced.

Chinese Writing

The earliest forms of Chinese characters, from around 1500 B.C. or earlier, were simplified pictures of things or ideas: ⊙ "sun," "horse," 馬 ﹒ "up," ﹣ "down." The written form of these characters changed greatly over time; they took on their modern form around A.D. 100, by which time the Chinese had invented paper. The technique of writing on paper with a small brush led to the characters being stylized and squared off; the modern form of the four words just given is 日 , 馬 , 上 , and 下 .

Very early in the history of Chinese writing, some characters began to be used as loan characters to write other words that sounded the same way. This quickly became confusing, however, so compound characters were created. A compound was formed from two parts: a "radical" or "signifier" that indicated the general subject to which the word referred, and a phonetic element to indicate the sound of the character. Thus all the words in a single sound group could be told apart. For example:

This meant that the written Chinese language played a very important role in binding the Chinese people together, throughout a large and diverse country. It also served to cement the ties between China and some smaller neighboring countries in China's cultural and political sphere of influence. Both Korea and Vietnam were separate countries, with languages quite unlike Chinese; both used classical Chinese as their written language for official documents and important works of literature. Japanese writing, in a more complex way, is also based on written Chinese.

Phonetic	Radical	(Explanation)	Compound
葉 "dyeh" +	虫 "insect"	(the *dyeh* word that refers to insects)	蝶 *dyeh*, "butterfly"
葉 "dyeh" +	金 "metal"	(the *dyeh* word that refers to metal)	鍱 *dyeh*, "thin metal plates"

Because the pronunciation of Chinese has evolved greatly over the centuries, Chinese characters today are only loosely phonetic; only sometimes it is possible to tell from their written form approximately how they should be pronounced. But meaning is embedded in the written words themselves, regardless of pronunciation. One way to understand how this works is to think about numbers. Take, for example, the number 3. Whether you pronounce it "three," or "drei," or "tres," or "san," neither its written form nor its meaning changes. Similarly, the Chinese character 永 conveys the meaning "eternity," whether one pronounces it "yong" (in Mandarin) or "wing" (in Cantonese). You could, if you wanted to, pronounce it "eternity."

The reverence and respect that Chinese culture gives to the written word goes far beyond the simple usefulness of communicating in writing. In part, respect for writing is tied to respect for the past: It is through the written word that the classical literature of poetry, philosophy, and history has been preserved. This literature forms an almost sacred record of the history of the Middle Kingdom, and a precious legacy from previous generations. In recognition of this, the most important single criterion for government service in premodern China was literacy and a knowledge of classical literature. In addition, Chinese characters were valued for their own sake, and characters written in beautiful calligraphy were regarded as the highest form of art.

From the traditional Chinese point of view, no person could be regarded as truly civilized without being literate in Chinese. Because China was seen as the world's unique source of civilization, any "barbarian" who wished to be considered civilized had, first of all, to learn Chinese.

You Are What You Eat

Literate or not, everyone in China also applied other criteria for what it meant to be a person of the Middle Kingdom. One of the most important of these was a proper diet.

Plowing a rice paddy with a water buffalo, Hunan Province. For thousands of years the growing of grain has been the basis of the Chinese way of life.

Quite simply, a civilized diet consists of *fan* and *cai*. *Fan* means "cooked rice," or by extension, any cooked grain; *cai*, literally "vegetables," means any food cut into bite-sized pieces (suitable for eating with chopsticks) and cooked to be eaten along with grain. *Cai* might, if one is poor, be very humble and meagre; but no meal is complete without a substantial quantity of rice, or noodles, or steamed bread, or even gruel. Judging from cooking vessels found in archaeological sites from the earliest stages of Chinese culture, this definition of a proper diet has always been part of being Chinese.

For centuries, Chinese people told one another stories about the disgusting foods eaten by the barbarians beyond the edges of the Middle Kingdom: in the north, large hunks of grilled meat, and various forms of "rotted milk" (i.e., cheese and yogurt); in the west, all of those things, plus roasted cracked barley mixed with butter. In the south, people at least ate rice, but that was not enough to make up for the large quantities of tubers, tropical fruit, and wild game in their diets. Chinese officials who were sent on missions to such places made great efforts to continue to eat in Chinese style and felt miserable when they could not.

The necessity of eating a grain-based diet put practical limits on the expansion of the Middle Kingdom. For Chinese people would not settle in places where it was not possible to live as Chinese, and peoples on the periphery whose life-styles were incompatible with that of the Chinese could not be accepted as people of the Middle Kingdom. The forests of the northeast, the mountains and deserts of the north and west, the mountains and tropical forests of the south, all were unsuitable for growing grain, and thus marked the natural limits of China's expansion. China did try repeatedly over a period of many centuries to absorb two areas in which no natural barriers to grain agriculture exist: northern Korea and northern Vietnam; they were held back only by the resistance to conquest of the people of those countries. Small outposts

An Ancient Feast

In the third-century-B.C. poem "Jao Hun" ("Summons to the Soul"), the narrator tries to call the soul of a dead person back to his body by offering a life of royal luxury, including a splendid feast:

> *Oh soul, return! Why should you go far away?*
> *Your household has gathered in your honor; all sorts of good*
>   *food is ready:*
> *Rice, sorghum, winter wheat, mixed with yellow millet;*
> *Bitter, salty, sour, hot, and sweet—there are dishes of*
>   *every flavor;*
> *Ribs of fattened beef, tender and juicy; sour-pungent soup*
>   *in the Wu style;*
> *Turtle stew and roast lamb with yam sauce; geese cooked*
>   *in sour sauce;*
> *Potted duck, fried crane, braised chicken; boiled tortoise,*
>   *highly spiced and full of flavor.*
> *There are fried rice-flour honey-cakes, and malt-sugar candy.*
> *Jade-pure wine, flavored with honey, fills the wing-handled*
>   *cups;*
> *Iced wine, well strained, clear, cool, and refreshing;*
> *Here are the lacquer-painted ladles, here is the sparkling wine.*
> *Oh soul, come back.*

Note that the meal begins with cooked grain—*fan*—and continues with a rich variety of side dishes—*cai*—accompanied by wine.

of Chinese civilization were also established in the oases of Central Asia —where little grain could be grown—to handle trade along the Silk Route and to defend that strategic corridor.

In fact, the Great Wall of China, first built in the third century B.C. and reconstructed many times thereafter, can be seen as much as a cultural boundary as a fortification. In effect, it says to the nomadic horsemen to the north of China, "You stay outside of the wall and raise animals; we will stay inside the wall and grow grain. If we each keep in our place, we can live at peace." The wall's serpentine route across northern China tends to follow fairly well the boundary (determined by climate and soil) of the feasible cultivation of grain by traditional methods.

In addition to the question of a proper diet, the Chinese applied other similar tests of cultural identity. For example, it was said that barbarians fastened their clothing on the "wrong" side of the body, and wore their hair loose, rather than neatly tied in a bun like the Chinese. In themselves these distinctions may seem trivial, but they provided additional ways of discovering whether or not people conformed to commonly accepted cultural standards of what it meant to be Chinese.

Notice that all of these definitions of "Chineseness" are cultural, and not racial or ethnic. Of course, the Chinese accepted as normal the kind of physical appearance that they were used to seeing; actually, they rarely encountered people whose hair color, skin color, and eye shape was radically different from their own. When they did meet West Asians or Europeans, Africans or people from the Asian tropics, they were quite surprised to see red hair and blue eyes, curly hair and dark skin —and they found those features very unattractive. A blond European might never be accepted as being Chinese—the contradiction in appearance is too obvious—but he could learn to become cultured and civilized by Chinese standards, and thus be accepted as a functioning member

of Chinese society. The gene pool of the Chinese people today contains contributions from ancestors of a variety of ethnic groups, absorbed through generations of intermarriage.

The Great Family

Every Chinese sees himself or herself as part of a lineage extending from the past into the future. The family, rather than the individual, is the basic unit of society. The family is not regarded as a static unit at a moment in time, but part of an ongoing continuum. Ancestors are venerated, and it is a sacred obligation to produce descendants. This explains the importance of sons in Chinese society: Descent is through the male line, and a family that produces no son ceases to exist. The concept of the family provides another set of social norms for being Chinese.

First, the family provides a model for society as a whole. The relationship between a father and a son is seen as the key to a society that is both hierarchical and harmonious, in which everyone knows his place and behaves accordingly. The father-son relationship is not one between equal individuals, but between a superior and an inferior. The father owes his son education, discipline, protection, and a model for behavior; the son owes his father respect and obedience no matter what (even if the father fails to live up to his own obligations). This deference is owed not only to the father, but to the entire line of male ancestors.

The father-son relationship provides the model for the other four of what the Chinese call "the five social bonds": ruler-subject, husband-

The Great Wall, near Beijing. The wall, marking the boundary between Chinese agriculture and "barbarian" grazing lands, was built in the third century B.C. and reconstructed in the fifteenth century A.D. A few small sections of the wall have been restored in recent years, but most of it now lies in ruins.

What's in a Name?

The structure of Chinese names emphasizes the importance of the family over that of the individual: Traditionally, names have been given in the order surname + personal name. Thus Wang Yufan, for example, would be the name of a member of the Wang family whose personal name is Yufan. Among members of the elite in premodern times, the question of names could become quite complex, as a single individual might be known by several different names under different circumstances. A child would be given, first, a childhood name, used within the family and among playmates. When the child reached puberty, the childhood name would be discarded, and he or she would be given an adult personal name, to be used throughout adulthood. In early adulthood, that personal name would be supplemented by a "public name"; the latter, which often expressed some ideal quality for which the person wished to be known, was used by friends and professional associates. Artists and writers also commonly chose a "studio name" or *nom de plume*, with which they signed their works.

For example, the best-known poet of the Song Dynasty was Su Shi; his surname was Su, and his adult personal name was Shi. He also used the "public name" Zizhan, meaning "Respectful Disciple"; and he signed many of his poems "Dongpo," meaning "Eastern Hillside," after the location of his country house. Thus Su Shi, Su Zizhan, and Su Dongpo are three different names for the same person.

The names of Chinese emperors are a special case. The rebel leader who founded the Han Dynasty was named Liu Bang, but he is known to history as Han Gaozu, the "High Ancestor of Han." That name, however, was unknown during his lifetime; it is a posthumous name assigned for use in ancestral sacrifices in his honor. His great-grandson, the sixth Han emperor (reigned 140–86 B.C.) was given the posthumous temple name Shizong, "Era Progenitor," but he is more commonly known to history by his (also posthumous) "canonical name," Han Wuti, "Martial Emperor of the Han."

The personal names of Chinese emperors were taboo, and were never spoken or written in public. During an emperor's lifetime he was known by his "reign-period name." This was not, strictly speaking, a name for the emperor at all, but rather the name of the period during which he ruled. In ancient times the reign-period name might change several times during an emperor's years on the throne; a new reign period might be announced, for example, to inaugurate a new imperial initiative or to change, magically, a run of imperial bad luck.

During the Ming and Qing dynasties, the custom of changing reign-period names was abandoned, and an emperor chose a single name for the entire reign. Thus, Ming and Qing emperors are always known historically by their reign-period names. Such names are always given in the form "The Qianlong Emperor" (meaning "the emperor who ruled during the Qianlong—'heavenly-exalted'—reign period"); the form "Emperor Qianlong" is incorrect, because Qianlong is the name not of the person, but of his reign.

Citizens of all ethnic groups march forward beneath a portrait of Chairman Mao Zedong. Chinese propaganda posters frequently emphasize that China is a multi-ethnic nation, but the extent to which minority ethnic groups share a sense of Chinese nationality is open to question.

behavior. When, in the nineteenth century, China came under pressure from the nations of the west to accept western standards of international relations between sovereign nations, the definition of China itself had to change. "All under heaven" became the nation-state of China, with borders defined by lines drawn clearly on a map. Anyone living within those lines—whether Chinese or not, in terms of culture—became a citizen of China.

About 95 percent of the people of China regard themselves as Chinese by any standard—racial, ethnic, or cultural. These are the Han people, as they call themselves, the cultural heirs of the great civilization that arose on the North China Plain thousands of years ago and spread throughout the Middle Kingdom. For this vast majority, citizenship in a nation called China simply reinforces their own cultural self-identity. This is as true on Taiwan as it is on the mainland. But for the remaining 5 percent—more than fifty million people—the question of citizenship and identity is important, and sometimes troubling.

The boundaries of China today incorporate far more territory than was traditionally included in the Middle Kingdom. Enormous areas, especially in the north, west, and southwest, include large numbers of people in many different groups who had never been regarded as Chinese, either by the Han people or by themselves. They include Mongols, Uighurs, Kazakhs, Tibetans, Miao, and many others. By language, diet, dress, social customs, and so on, they are not Chinese, but they are citizens of China.

The government of the People's Republic of China has instituted a set of policies for these so-called "national minorities" that are designed to resolve the tension between cultural identity and national citizenship. At least in theory, China is to be a culturally pluralistic society, in which the culture of the Han majority and the cultures of the various national minorities are to be equally respected. Culture and citizenship are to be seen as compatible parts of one's identity, rather than being in conflict. Members of minority groups are allowed a substantial amount of local autonomy, while owing national allegiance to the People's Republic. This theoretical autonomy, however, has been seriously compromised by the government's insistence that "feudal" aspects of traditional minority culture be suppressed.

The national minorities are themselves very diverse. Some include millions of people, occupying vast territories; others include only a few thousand people in a handful of villages. Some are culturally quite similar to the Chinese: The Hui national minority, for example, includes millions of people who would be regarded as Han in all respects but one,

Ethnic Map: The Peoples of China

Sino-Tibetan
Han (Chinese)
Tibeto-Burman
Tai-Mon Khmer
Miao-Yao
Altaic
Turkic
Mongolian
Korean
Area outlined in black uninhabited

China: Ethnic/Linguistic Distribution. Cities, towns, and some agricultural areas in non-Han regions contain sizeable Han populations as a result of internal migration. The Hui (Han Muslim) ethnic minority is widely distributed in pockets throughout northern, western, and southwestern China.

that they are Muslims. By adopting Islam, they have defined themselves as being separate from the Chinese people in beliefs and diet (for example, they abstain from eating pork), but otherwise they look Chinese, speak Chinese, and accept most of the norms of Chinese culture. Other minorities are radically different from the Chinese. Tibetans have a strong sense of national identity, based on a particular type of Buddhism known as Lamaism and reinforced by language, dress, diet, and other cultural factors. Many Tibetans would not agree that Tibet should be politically part of China at all, and there is a Tibetan government-in-exile, headed by the Dalai Lama, in India.

The policy of the Chinese government has been to encourage cultural awareness and autonomy among the national minority peoples, but to refuse absolutely to permit any expression of cultural nationalism. But even cultural autonomy is difficult to maintain. Members of the smaller minority groups especially find it difficult to resist the subtle cultural signals of the Chinese majority that say, in effect, "To behave this way is civilized, to behave that way is barbaric. Wouldn't you like to be civilized, like us?" And in fact, many members of minority groups in China have now become largely assimilated into the Han majority, continuing a process that has gone on for centuries. But for minority peoples who have no wish to assimilate, and for their Han neighbors, the question of citizenship and identity will continue to be an awkward and unsolvable problem.

The concept of citizenship certainly does not play a large role in the modern definition of Han identity. If you regard yourself as Chinese, and are accepted by other Chinese as being Chinese, then you *are* Chinese. And "once Chinese, always Chinese." A completely Americanized Chinese American whose great-grandparents were born in the United States might be criticized by more culturally traditional Chinese people—"He has forgotten how to be Chinese"—but the definition of

Chineseness comes at least as much from one's ancestors as from one's self. A person whose ancestors were Chinese will be regarded by most other Chinese as being Chinese, whether he or she lives in London, Nairobi, or Beijing, and regardless of the citizenship that he or she claims. In today's world, China is a nation, but *Zhongguo,* "The Middle Kingdom," remains an idea that has become part of our global heritage.

The Land

The total land area of China is roughly the same as that of the United States. That equal amount of land, however, must provide food for nearly five times as many people. The problem is even more severe than this simple comparison would suggest, for China has significantly less land than the United States that is suitable for agriculture. Most of the territory of China is mountainous, arid, or both.

China is a land of great geographical diversity, with climate zones ranging from alpine and subarctic to tropical, with the world's highest mountain and the world's second-lowest desert depression, with three of the world's longest rivers and one of the world's driest deserts. It has the world's largest and highest dry plateau, and two of the world's largest fertile river basins. The landscape of China includes areas of spectacular, wild natural beauty; it also contains vast areas that have been completely transformed from their natural state by the agricultural labor of a hundred generations.

It is useful to think of China as consisting of the agricultural heartland—the traditional realm of the Chinese emperors, and home of the Chinese people—plus vast "barbarian" outlying territories that the Chinese emperors sought to control for political and/or military reasons, and which were included with China when modern national

China's Geographical Diversity

Highest Mountain	Mount Qomolangma (Mount Everest): 29,028 feet (8848 meters)
Lowest Depression	Turfan Depression: 501 feet (153 meters) below sea level
Longest Rivers	Chang Jiang (Yangtse): 3494 miles (5660 kilometers)
	Huang He (Yellow River): 2903 miles (4670 kilometers)
Largest Lakes	Boyang: up to 1950 square miles (5050 square kilometers); varies seasonally
	Qinghai: 1709 square miles (4427 square kilometers)
Most Rainfall	Southern coast of Guangxi Province, Gulf of Tonkin: about 110 inches (280 centimeters) per year
Least Rainfall	Taklamakan Desert: Less than 4 inches (10 centimeters) per year

boundaries were drawn on the map of the world in the nineteenth century.

The Heartland

Roughly speaking, the territory of "China proper" includes the lands south of the Great Wall, east of the Tibetan Plateau, and north of the mountain ranges and tropical forests of Burma, Laos, and Vietnam. This, in other words, is the Middle Kingdom, the traditional Chinese heartland in which the growing of grain has formed the basis of society throughout history. This heartland includes much less than half the total area of the People's Republic of China, but supports nearly 90 percent of the population. Even this heartland includes large mountainous areas that are not arable, but in general the Middle Kingdom is a human landscape, dedicated to the intensive production of grain.

The heartland may be thought of as comprising three subregions, each having distinctive geographical and agricultural characteristics. They are North China, South China, and the Sichuan Basin. North and South China are divided along a line that roughly follows the course of the Han and Huai rivers; the Sichuan Basin is bounded on the north, east, and south by mountain ranges, and on the west by the Tibetan Plateau.

North China   The north is dominated by the Yellow River and its tributaries, but despite the enormous amount of water that flows through these rivers (fed by snow-covered mountains farther west), the terrain is quite dry. Rainfall is irregular and often inadequate. In compensation for this dryness, however, the north is covered by a very fertile and easily worked type of soil called loess.

Loess is actually a yellowish-brown dust, blown from what is now the

Physical Map: Topography

dry, stony Gobi Desert by cyclonic winds at the end of the last Ice Age, about 12,000 years ago. For centuries the winds blew, picking up dust and then, as the winds lost energy, dropping it over northwestern China. In parts of Shaanxi Province, deposits of loess are over 200 feet thick. The structure of loess particles is such that this soil erodes easily and tends to form steep cliffs, so northwestern China is marked by eroded hills and deep, naturally-terraced river valleys. Loess is very fertile, as the earliest Neolithic Chinese farmers discovered when they cultivated millet along the river terraces of northwestern China 7000 years ago. It also makes a good building material; many Chinese even today live comfortably in houses cut into the face of loess cliffs.

Loess hills along the Yellow River in Shaanxi Province. The terraced fields in the foreground are typical of modern efforts to control erosion and create new farmland.
Courtesy of Chinese People's Association for Friendship with Foreign Countries.

The Yellow River takes its name from the huge quantities of eroded loess that it transports toward the sea. At flood stage the water of the Yellow River can contain as much as 20 percent silt, by volume. As the river emerges from the mountain passes of the northwest, it broadens and slows down, and the silt is deposited in the riverbed. Because the bottom of the river continually rises, its course is very unstable. The Yellow River has flooded hundreds of times since the last Ice Age, depositing a fresh layer of loess mud each time over thousands of square miles, and then cutting a new course to the sea. In fact the mouth of the river has shifted drastically several times during recorded history, sometimes lying north of the Shandong Peninsula and sometimes south of it.

The floods of the Yellow River have created the North China Plain, a mostly level landscape covering large portions of the provinces of Shanxi, Shandong, Hebei, and Henan. The soil—loess silt—is very rich, and this plain is heavily settled and cultivated. From an airplane flying over the North China Plain, one sees a seemingly endless landscape of cultivated fields, dotted at half-mile intervals with small villages. Although irrigation has made it possible to create extensive paddy fields in some parts of this region for the cultivation of rice, the main crops of North China are open-field grains, such as wheat, corn, sorghum, and millet. Other important crops are cotton, green vegetables, and orchard fruits such as persimmons (in the northwest) and pears (in the mountainous peninsula of Shandong).

In a sense, the North China Plain and the adjacent Wei River Valley are the heartland of the heartland. From about 1000 B.C. to A.D. 1000, the capital of China was almost always either at Chang'an (Xi'an) or Luoyang. Since 1279, the capital has usually been at Beijing, close to the strategically vital northern frontier. Some of the cities of North China, such as Zhengzhou and Kaifeng, are also very ancient; others, such as Tianjin, Qingdao, and Jinan, have developed greatly in modern times as centers of transportation and industry.

South China

South China   South of the Han-Huai dividing line, loess gives way to more ancient and less fertile soils. There is, however, more abundant water, as much of southern China receives regular, seasonal rains. The Chang Jiang ("Long River," usually known in the West by its alternate name, the Yangtse) is the world's third-longest river; its floodplain and delta are fertile and well watered, and Jiangsu and Zhejiang provinces are known as "the rice bowl of China." Beyond the Chang Jiang Valley, South China is hilly or mountainous. Settlement and transportation have followed the numerous river valleys of the region. Whereas villages in North China appear as clusters on the plain, those in South China tend to be strung out along rivers or canals. Hillsides are terraced for rice paddies wherever possible; water is provided by elaborate irrigation works, and annual applications of manure and other fertilizers lend help to the generally impoverished soil.

Rice is the main crop of South China; in some areas two or even three crops can be grown every year. Some fields are used to grow a summer crop of rice and a winter crop of wheat. Green vegetables, oilseed, and tobacco are also important crops. Many hillsides of southeastern China are covered by extensive plantations of tea bushes. And in the Chang Jiang Valley, roadsides, riverbanks, and other marginal lands not used for paddy fields are commonly planted with mulberry trees, the young green leaves of which provide food for silkworms. Large citrus orchards are found in the valley of the Xiang River and other tributaries of the central Chang Jiang. In the far south, one finds bananas and other tropical fruits.

In contrast to the generally dry climate of the north, South China is hot and humid in the summer and cold and damp in the winter. Rain

may fall at any time of the year, but it is concentrated in the spring and early summer, as part of the monsoon climate system of southern Asia. Again in contrast to the north, which is generally deficient in minerals except for coal, iron, and a few petroleum deposits, South China has significant mineral resources, especially of such metals as lead, mercury, and tungsten.

The cities of South China have developed as trading and transportation centers, in ancient times on rivers (Wuhan, Nanjing) or, in more recent times, as international ports (Shanghai, Guangzhou [Canton], Fuzhou).

The mountainous areas of southern and southwestern China are home to several of China's national minorities. These peoples retreated to marginal areas as the territory under Chinese control expanded southward over the course of history.

The islands of Taiwan and Hainan are also included within South China, but they were marginal territories until relatively recent times. Significant Han migration to the islands began in the seventeenth century; there are still also minority populations of the original Malayo-Polynesian peoples on both islands today.

The Sichuan Basin

"Sichuan" means "four rivers," and the geography of the Sichuan Basin is dominated by the Chang Jiang and its main tributaries. By virtue of its fertile and well-watered soil, Sichuan Province has become home to 10 percent of China's population: 100 million people. The landscape is dominated by diked fields interlaced with innumerable streams and irrigation channels; in spring the brilliant green of young rice plants dazzles the eye. The countryside is dotted with farmsteads surrounded by graceful groves of bamboo. Rice

Water mill and rice paddies, Gueizhou Province. Terraced fields and irrigation channels are typical of the South China landscape, transformed by centuries of human effort.

and wheat are grown in rotation, along with vegetables, tobacco, mulberry trees, and orchard fruit. Sichuan has long been one of China's richest regions, as well as one of the most beautiful.

The Sichuan Basin has supported flourishing human communities since prehistoric times. Chengdu, the provincial capital, has a long history as an administrative and cultural center; the province's other large city, Chongqing, is a trading center and river port. The Dujiangyan irrigation system, near Chengdu, was first constructed around 250 B.C. and is still in use today. Mining and drilling for minerals are also ancient activities. Deep brine wells (for salt production) and natural gas wells were drilled as early as 2000 years ago, and coal, copper, silver, and other minerals are found in significant quantities in the surrounding mountains.

Animals of the Heartland

Traditionally, meat has played only a supplementary role in the Chinese diet; most people are likely to rely more on soybeans than on meat for the protein they need. Still, throughout China proper, pigs and ducks (both of which require relatively little space) are typically found on small farms. In recent times fish farming has emerged as an important activity in regions where there is enough water to supply artificial ponds. Horses, donkeys, and oxen are used as draft animals in North China; in Sichuan and the south, they are replaced by water buffalos. Nowadays agriculture is becoming mechanized in China, and tractors are increasingly common; but no tractor can maneuver as easily in a narrow, terraced rice paddy as a water buffalo can.

The Northeast

China's three northeastern provinces, collectively known as Manchuria, have long been a contested area between the Middle Kingdom and indigenous non-Chinese peoples. The lowland southern and central parts of the region are well suited to agriculture, particularly open-field crops of spring wheat and soybeans. They were, therefore, a natural target of Chinese territorial expansion at times when the empire had adequate political and military strength. Even during expansionist phases, however, the Chinese showed little interest in the heavily forested mountains and broad valleys that occupy the eastern and northern portions of Manchuria. The region was primarily populated by people who spoke a variety of Mongolian and Tungusic languages; the life-style of the inhabitants of the Manchurian lowlands was an extension of that of the Mongolian grasslands to the west. In the northern forests extending to and beyond the Heilongjiang (Amur River), smaller tribes lived by hunting or reindeer herding.

The northeastern provinces became permanently attached to the Chinese empire in the seventeenth century, when a confederation of Manchu-speaking tribes conquered China and stayed on to establish a Chinese-style government, the Qing Dynasty, at the same time bringing their own homeland into the realm. The Manchu conquest of China was sudden, military, and superficial; the Chinese conquest of Manchuria was long-term, largely peaceful, and thorough. Beginning in the late nineteenth century, large numbers of Han immigrants moved to the northeast to exploit the high-grade deposits of coal and iron that have since made Liaoning and Jilin provinces among China's most important industrial regions. Today the population of the northeast is overwhelmingly Han; Manchu is a dying language. The old Manchu capital of Mukden has been overwhelmed by and absorbed into the great industrial city of Shenyang; the other cities of the region, too—such as Changchun and Dalian—are products of the modern era, centers of industry and trade. The Daqing oilfields, near Harbin, hold some of China's most important petroleum reserves. Forestry forms the basis for the region's economy outside the industrial lowlands.

Geographically, the northeast is dominated by the broad valley of the Sungari River. The Sungari flows into the Amur River, which forms the boundary between China and the Soviet Union; another tributary of the Amur, the Ussuri, forms the China-U.S.S.R. boundary on the east. Farther south, the Yalu and Tumen rivers define the boundary between China and North Korea. These river systems have a substantial hydro-electric power potential, still only partly developed. In general, the northeast is amply supplied with water. Except near the coast, the climate is harsh, with long, severe winters.

The Northern Frontier

The western boundary of Manchuria is marked by the Xing'an (Khing-an) Mountains, a great mountain range that runs from the Amur River to the coast of Liaoning Province, northeast of Beijing. The point where the mountains meet the sea (called, appropriately, Shanhaiguan, "mountain-sea barrier") is also the eastern terminus of the Great Wall. From there, the wall meanders westward for over 1000 miles, marking the approximate boundary between northern grasslands, where nomads on horseback tend their flocks of sheep, and southern arable fields. The present boundary between China and the Mongolian People's Republic lies well north of the wall, and is the result of a modern political settlement. In recent times agriculture, too, has spread north of the wall, with the aid of irrigation and mechanization. Nevertheless, most of the northern frontier region is high, open country, with terrain ranging from rich grasslands to arid prairie to barren desert. In general, the climate becomes steadily drier as one moves from east to west, away from the coast.

The Great Wall cuts across the big northerly bend of the Yellow River, isolating the grasslands of the Ordos Plateau. The Ordos region holds vast deposits of coal, which have led to the growth of the city of Baotou as a major industrial center. Politically, most of the northern frontier region of China is incorporated into the Inner Mongolian Autonomous Region, which borders the Mongolian People's Republic to the north. Following the ancient life-style of pastoral nomadism, the Mongol inhabitants of the region learn to ride even before they can walk. Every year they drive flocks of sheep from pasture to pasture in a regular seasonal pattern, riding horses or camels and living in felt tents called yurts. The great fairs at which the tribes gather every year to buy and sell their animals are festivals of singing, dancing, horse-racing, archery contests, and wrestling. In the twentieth century the Mongol population of China north of the wall has come to be outnumbered by Han immigrants, drawn to the cities of Baotou and Huhete and to scattered agricultural settlements.

The Northwest and Xinjiang

From the city of Lanzhou, capital of Gansu Province, a narrow corridor of arable land points north-westward, rising in gentle stages to the plains of Central Asia. Marked by scattered towns and villages and marginal fields of oats and barley, bounded on the south by the Nan Shan Range and protected on the north by the western reaches of the Great Wall, the Gansu Corridor was for centuries China's only reliable overland link with Central Asia, India, and the Middle East. Camel caravans laden with bales of silk cloth left Lanzhou and followed the

Beijing, 1939: A camel caravan sets out for Inner Mongolia. Caravans like this one carried most long-distance trade in northern China for 2000 years.

Silk Route through the corridor and across Asia, all the way to Damascus. Passing the Jade Gate at the western border of Gansu Province—the last outpost of the Middle Kingdom—they entered Xinjiang (literally, the "New Frontier").

Now known as the Xinjiang Uighur Autonomous Region, China's northwestern frontier is huge, with an area almost twice the size of California, Oregon, and Washington combined. Xinjiang has been politically part of China since the Qing Dynasty; the present borders between China and Russia were defined in the nineteenth century. Physically and culturally, however, the northwest is remote from the Chinese heartland.

Xinjiang is bounded by two mountain ranges, the Altai Mountains on the Mongolian border in the north, and in the south the Kunlun Range, which forms the north wall of the Tibetan Plateau. The region is divided in half by the Tianshan Range, which extends eastward from the Pamir Mountains of eastern Afghanistan and terminates abruptly at Xinjiang's Turfan Depression, more than 500 feet below sea level. The portion of Xinjiang north of the Tianshan Range is also known as Dzungaria; its terrain varies from grasslands to desert, dotted with oases. Flocks of sheep and goats and herds of camels and horses are raised in scattered pastures. Oasis towns like Hami and Turpan, which formerly served as way stations on the Silk Route, are now famous for growing melons, grapes, and dates. Urumqi, the region's capital and only large city, is an industrial center, drawing on Xinjiang's resources of coal, petroleum, and minerals.

Oasis village, western Gansu Province. The temple in the left background has a Chinese-style roof; otherwise, both the terrain and the architecture are more typical of Central Asia than of the heartland of the Middle Kingdom.

South of the Tianshan Range are the Taklamakan Desert and the Tarim Basin, huge, barren, and almost unpopulated wastelands. Ancient caravan routes through this area skirted the foothills of either the Tianshan or the Kunlun ranges, converging on the oasis city of Kashi (Kashgar), one of the crossroads of Central Asia.

The population of Xinjiang consists mainly of Turkic-speaking Uighurs and Kazakhs, with smaller numbers of Mongols, Tibetans, and other non-Han peoples. In recent decades, however, large numbers of Han Chinese have migrated to Urumqi and some of the larger oasis towns.

Tibet

Historically and culturally Tibet has included not only the present Tibet Autonomous Region but also Qinghai Province and much of western Sichuan. Bounded on the north by the Kunlun Mountains and on the south by the Himalayas, Tibet is by far the world's largest and highest plateau, with elevations generally above 13,000 feet. Since the Tang Dynasty, China has incorporated Tibet into its empire whenever it had the diplomatic and military strength to do so; Tibet, on the other hand, has asserted its independence whenever possible.

Barley, the only grain that grows well at high altitude, is the staple of the Tibetan diet. Although it is ringed by snow-covered mountains, most of the Tibetan Plateau is a cold desert, so agriculture is also limited by the scarcity of water. Sheep and yaks are raised for meat, milk, and wool; yaks are also used as pack animals. Most of the territory is very thinly inhabited. The capital, Lhasa, and a few other large towns are concentrated in southern Tibet. For centuries, yak caravans have traveled south from those towns, through the Himalayan passes, with cargos of animal products, gold, and turquoise, returning laden with salt and tea.

Culture often follows trade, and Tibet's most important cultural ties are to Nepal and northern India. The Tibetan language is distantly related to Chinese, but it is written with an alphabet derived from Sanskrit, the ancient language of India. The Buddhist religion, which originated in southern Nepal, has evolved in Tibet into a distinctive sect called Lamaism, which has played a dominant role in the lives of the Tibetan people. Tibet's incorporation into the People's Republic of China has been marked by periodic outbreaks of violent protest followed by military repression.

The Southwest

The eastern foothills of the Himalayas, occupying parts of Sichuan and Yunnan provinces and bordering on Burma and Laos, form China's southwestern frontier region. Some of Asia's greatest rivers—including the Chang Jiang, the Red River, the Mekong (called the Lancang in China), and the Salween—have their sources in eastern Tibet or the foothills to the east, and flow in nearly parallel steep valleys through southwestern China before spreading out like the ribs of a fan to meet the ocean at the East China Sea, the South China Sea, and the Bay of Bengal.

The steep mountains of the southwest, covered by tropical forests, are home to many of China's ethnic minority groups, such as the Yao, the Miao, the Dai, and the Lahu. These peoples, distinguished from the Han Chinese and from each other by differences in language, costume, and beliefs, nevertheless tend to follow a roughly uniform life-style. Living in small villages, they plant yams and vegetables, and grow rice in terraced paddy fields or on open hillsides. The main domestic animals are pigs and water buffalo. Formerly almost completely isolated from the outside world, the region has now been made accessible by a

network of roads. As a result, timber, food crops, and such minerals as jade, tin, copper, and tungsten have grown in economic importance. The city of Kunming, capital of Yunnan Province, serves as a metropolitan center for both the Han majority and the numerous national minorities of the region.

The southwest has a long history of cultural distinctiveness. The Bronze Age Dongson culture of the Red River Valley dates back to at least 2500 years ago. It was well known to the Chinese to the north, and extended its cultural influence as far afield as Indonesia, where unique Dongson bronze drums have been found in archaeological excavations. Modern political boundaries in the region artificially cut across a larger cultural area; the minority peoples of southwestern China have strong cultural ties with the mountain-dwelling peoples of northeastern India, Burma, Thailand, Laos, and Vietnam.

The climate of the southwest ranges from subtropical to tropical, with hot summers, mild winters, and abundant rainfall. Kunming is known in China as "the city of perpetual springtime."

City and Country

Although more than 200 million people—almost as many as the entire population of the United States—live in China's cities and large towns, China remains an overwhelmingly rural country: another 800 million people live in the countryside. Historically, cities and towns served primarily as administrative centers, and secondarily as centers of commerce, manufacturing, scholarship, and the arts. They spread a thin net

This young Buddhist monk in Xishuangbanna, southern Yunnan Province, is a member of the Dai nationality. Despite pressure from the Han majority, many of China's minority ethnic groups retain their own religion, dress, and customs.

of national unity over a country where local and regional interests (and in frontier areas, ethnic interests) tended to dominate.

China's regional diversity was compounded by the difficulties of long-distance transportation before modern times. China's major rivers mostly flow from west to east, facilitating travel in those directions, particularly on the Chang Jiang and its tributaries. (Wuhan, for example, is a port for oceangoing ships, even though it is 600 miles upriver from the coast.) In the eastern part of the country, north-south travel was aided by the construction, around A.D. 600, of the Grand Canal, designed to allow grain barges to travel from the Chang Jiang Delta to Chang'an. In the thirteenth century a northern spur was added, terminating near Beijing. Throughout the country, however, overland travel in any direction was usually difficult and time-consuming.

Today, a large and expanding national rail network covers most of the country, fostering both internal commerce and a sense of national unity. It is possible, for example, to take a through train from Shanghai to Urumqi, reducing to a few days a journey that might once have taken six months. National and regional air networks have also developed rapidly since 1949. Road transportation, however, remains mostly regional rather than national. Radio and television broadcasting, and nationally distributed newspapers, magazines, and motion pictures all now play an important role in reducing the differences between city and country, north and south, Han and non-Han, Middle Kingdom and frontier territories.

These two middle-level officials are members of the vast bureaucracy that governs modern China. The "Mao suit," standard dress for all Chinese until a few years ago, is now rapidly giving way to Western-style clothes, especially in China's cities.

Key Themes
in Chinese History

Studying Chinese History

China is not the world's oldest civilization, but it does have the longest continuous historical record of any society in the world. The civilizations and empires of the eastern Mediterranean and the Middle East rose and fell in dramatic succession. Pharaonic Egypt was buried by Greco-Roman civilization, which in turn was overwhelmed in Egypt by Islam. The story of civilization in China is one of change and evolution in an overall context of continuity for a period of over 4000 years.

An acute awareness of history is one of the most striking features of Chinese culture. Careful attention to historical record-keeping is almost as old as Chinese civilization itself; scholars today make use of archives preserved by the kings of the Shang Dynasty 3300 years ago. For over two thousand years, up until modern times, every Chinese dynasty has considered it a solemn obligation to compile an official history of the preceding dynasty. This devotion to the past had two sources. First, the veneration of ancestors—a central feature of Chinese culture—demanded that a record of past accomplishments should be kept and passed on to future generations. Second, the rulers of China believed that the kings and culture heros of the remote past (whether real or legendary) provided the best available models for human conduct, and that the past provided guidance for the present and the future. This attitude is summed up in the title of an encyclopedic history written in the eleventh century A.D.: "The Comprehensive Mirror for Aid in Government."

China's historical record is extraordinarily rich. It is contained in hundreds of thousands of printed volumes and in millions of objects, many of them recently recovered through archaeological excavations. The amount of knowledge contained in that record is overwhelming, and yet it does not tell the whole story. China's written history was compiled by the literate upper class, and has little to say about the interests and activities of farmers and workers, of women, of non-Han peoples. The information that is available on those subjects in the written record must be used with caution, because of the bias of its point of view. Many topics in Chinese history are still very imperfectly understood; new knowledge and new perspectives are constantly emerging as the work of historians and archaeologists continues.

A great deal of factual information must be mastered in trying to come to grips with thousands of years of Chinese history. It is important, however, to avoid becoming bogged down in a long parade of historical facts. It is helpful to think in terms of certain overarching themes that lend unity and coherence to the long sweep of Chinese history.

Periods of Chinese History

ca. 5000 B.C.	Neolithic Revolution in China
ca. 1953–1576 B.C.	Xia Kingdom
ca. 1576–1059 B.C.	Shang Dynasty
ca. 1059–221 B.C.	Zhou Dynasty
1059–770 B.C.	Western Zhou
770–481 B.C.	Spring and Autumn Period ⎤ (Eastern
403–221 B.C.	Warring States Period ⎦ Zhou)
221–206 B.C.	Qin Dynasty
206 B.C.–A.D. 220	Han Dynasty
206 B.C.–A.D. 7	Former Han, or Eastern Han
7–A.D. 23	Wang Mang Interregnum (Xin Dynasty)
23–A.D. 220	Latter Han, or Western Han
220–263	Three Kingdoms Period
263–589	Northern and Southern Dynasties (Period of Disunion)
263–317	Western Jin
317–420	Eastern Jin
386–534	Northern Wei
589–618	Sui Dynasty
618–907	Tang Dynasty
907–960	Five Dynasties
960–1279	Song Dynasty
960–1127	Northern Song
947–1125	Liao Dynasty
1127–1279	Southern Song
1125–1234	Jin Dynasty
1279–1368	Yuan Dynasty
1368–1644	Ming Dynasty
1644–1911	Qing Dynasty
1911–	Republic of China
1949–	People's Republic of China

The Dynastic Cycle

Most of Chinese history has been divided into periods defined by dynasties: families of rulers who, for a number of generations, occupied the Chinese throne. The first dynasty was the Xia, founded *ca.* 1953 B.C.; the last ended in A.D. 1911, with the abdication of China's last emperor. These kings (or, as they were called from the Qin Dynasty onward, emperors) were believed to have the right to rule because of the Mandate of Heaven. This said, in effect, that a king was king because he was so filled with virtue as to be in tune with the powers of the universe itself; his combination of personal goodness and cosmic power made everyone acknowledge him as king. But what about his sons and grandsons? Would they be supremely virtuous as well? The theory of the Mandate of Heaven balanced the competing claims of virtue and heredity. The original king—the founder of a dynasty—had the right to bequeath his throne to his heirs; but if those heirs engaged in serious and persistent wickedness, the powers of heaven would be withdrawn from them. This would pave the way for a new dynastic founder to arise.

Chinese historians traditionally saw history as going through an endless cycle of renewal and decline, through dynasty after dynasty. By means of his supreme virtue (and, more practically, by intelligence, energy, military genius, and good luck) a dynastic founder would establish a regime based on time-tested ancient principles of fairness, honor, and efficiency. For several generations his heirs would remain true to the founder's legacy, and would also rule well. Eventually, however, rulers would become lazy, corrupt, and self-indulgent, and the interests of the empire as a whole would be neglected. Popular rebellions would break out, becoming more and more serious until finally a new leader would fight his way to the top, oust the last emperor, and establish a cleansed new dynasty of his own. As a broad generalization, the dynastic cycle helps to explain, through the mechanism of periodic renewal, how

the Chinese were able to retain a consistent and continuous pattern of government for thousands of years.

Unity and Fragmentation

Taken together, the belief that China was the Middle Kingdom and that its ruler reigned by means of a Mandate of Heaven meant that China (or rather, "all under heaven") should always be unified under a single monarch. In fact, however, China was often divided into two or more competing realms. Sometimes this fragmentation lasted only a few years or decades, between the fall of one long-term dynasty and the consolidation of the subsequent one. On two occasions (the Warring States Period, from 403 to 221 B.C., and the Period of Disunion from A.D. 265 to 589) the fragmentation lasted for many lifetimes. Even so, prolonged periods of disunion were always regarded as unnatural as well as undesirable. Chinese political theory always stressed the idea that there should be one ruler and one realm. The tension between forces leading to unification and forces leading to fragmentation is one of the most important long-term themes in Chinese history.

The Key Role of the Northern Frontier   During the whole span of Chinese history, China was at times very open to contact with the outside world, and at other times turned in upon itself. These periods of contact and isolation form a long-term historical pattern that

Uncovering the past: Since 1974 Chinese archaeologists have been at work excavating an underground clay army that guards the eastern approaches to the tomb of the First Emperor of Qin, near Xi'an. The vast pits near the tomb, constructed in 210 B.C., contain more than 6000 larger-than-life-size clay soldiers. Nearly all the figures were severely damaged after centuries of burial; most of those in this picture have been carefully restored and returned to their original positions. R. Mellal/Sygma.

is only partly linked to the rise and fall of particular dynasties. But regardless of whether China was in a cosmopolitan or an isolationist phase, whether Chinese military power was projected far out along the Silk Route or forced to withdraw to within the Great Wall, China's most pressing problem of defense and foreign relations was its northern frontier. Despite the theoretical boundary line marked by the Great Wall, the northern frontier is a broad belt of marginal land. The grasslands north of the wall can be plowed; the cultivated fields south of the wall can be turned into grazing lands. For dynasty after dynasty, China's rulers tried to bring as much of that land under their control as possible, and at least to avoid losing it to the nomads to the north.

This modest house is built against the side of a Han Dynasty watchtower that guarded the Silk Route in western Gansu Province over 2,000 years ago.

Northern "barbarians" invaded the frontier countless times, and succeeded in conquering much of China on several occasions. But, as the Chinese say, "One can conquer China on horseback, but one cannot rule China from horseback." Even alien dynasties ruled in Chinese fashion, and defended the northern frontier against other nomadic tribes. The crucial strategic role of the northern frontier, and to a lesser extent the need to control the Silk Route corridor to Central Asia, meant that China's rulers looked inland, turning their backs on the sea.

Of course, this is only relatively true. Records of officially sponsored sea voyages of exploration date back to the fourth century B.C. China's armed forces always included a fleet of warships, and boats were indispensable to daily life and commerce in South China. At the height of Chinese maritime power, in the fifteenth century, imperial fleets sailed to the South China Sea, the Indian Ocean, and the eastern coast of Africa. But China's capital was usually in the north, near the strategic northern frontier, while China's best ports are mostly concentrated on the southeastern coast. China was seldom threatened from the sea, until the arrival of the Europeans, and so most emperors gave low priority to sea power. With rare exceptions, Chinese maritime ventures were mostly private, small scale, and mercantile. From the point of view of its rulers, China was a continental rather than an oceanic power.

Strategically Important Regions

In addition to defending the northern frontier, governments of China throughout history had to pay special attention to several key strategic regions. One of these was the Wei River Valley and the adjacent loess hills of Shaanxi Province. The issue here was not external invasion, but internal rebellion. From the overthrow of the Shang Dynasty by the Zhou people of Shaanxi in 1059 B.C. to the establishment of the Communist headquarters at Yenan in the 1930s, the rugged terrain of the northwest has provided a staging area for rebellions against Chinese rulers. Throughout history, a loss of political and military control in the northwest has been a sign that the ruling dynasty was in danger.

A second strategic region was the Chang Jiang Valley, and particularly the delta region. In ancient China, that area was relatively underpopulated. It took centuries of sustained human labor to drain the marshes and construct the irrigation works and terraced fields needed to realize fully the region's potential as China's main rice-producing area. By the Han Dynasty (206 B.C. to A.D. 220), the economic power of the Chang Jiang Valley was beginning to be felt, and by the Tang Dynasty (A.D. 618–907), the center of economic power (but not the seat of political authority) had shifted from the North China Plain to the Chang Jiang Delta. The main source of revenue for China's dynastic governments was a land tax, collected either in grain and silk cloth or in cash from the peasants' sale of those commodities. Control of this central rice-producing region thus became a top priority for China's rulers. The Grand Canal was constructed primarily to transport tax receipts of grain and silk northward to the capital, both to provide extra food for the population of northern China and, especially, to finance the heavy military expense of guarding the northern frontier and garrisoning the strategic northwest.

For most of Chinese history from the Han Dynasty onward, the production of salt (and sometimes also of iron and other important metals) was a government-regulated monopoly. Income from salt production was an important supplementary source of government revenue, second only to the land tax. The brine wells of Sichuan thus made that province another key economic region. Most of the grain grown in Sichuan was consumed locally, but its salt was transported throughout the country, except to coastal regions, where salt was produced locally

A brine well, Sichuan. The tower on the left supports the drill-string of bamboo with an iron bit; the windlass on the right is used to raise and lower the drill-string and, after completion of the well, to raise long, slender bamboo buckets full of brine. Wells were often over 1000 feet deep. This technology, similar to that now used for oil wells, was invented in China around 200 B.C. Reproduced from a nineteenth-century edition of *Tiangong Kaiwu* ("The Exploitation of the Works of Heaven"), a seventeenth-century encyclopedia of technology.

by the evaporation of sea water. The production, transportation, and taxation of salt was closely controlled by the government, and the loss of that source of wealth would seriously weaken a dynasty.

Innovation and Stability

One of the most remarkable features of Chinese history is the degree to which China's social and political structures were resistant to fundamental change. It was not that China did not change at all; but, at least until the twentieth century, change was slow and evolutionary rather than rapid and revolutionary.

At the same time, throughout its long and culturally stable history, China was a tremendously fertile source of technological innovation. Paper and printing, gunpowder, and the magnetic compass are just the most famous of the many inventions that China exported to the rest of the world long before modern times. Interestingly, the revolutionary impact of such inventions was felt more outside of China than in China itself. The Chinese used gunpowder for military weapons as well as for fireworks; but because Chinese warfare did not rely on fortified castles and heavy cavalry, gunpowder in China did not lead to the development of the siege cannon and personal firearms that changed the nature of warfare in Europe forever. Printing certainly led to an expansion of literacy in China, and an increase in the number of books in circulation, but hardly to the "information explosion" that rocked Europe after Gutenberg introduced the printing press there. Or, to take another example, the development of high-yield strains of rice and an efficient threshing machine in China in the twelfth century led to a great increase in China's agricultural wealth, but to little change in how that wealth was distributed and invested.

China was huge in geographic area and population, militarily and economically dominant in East Asia, and usually relatively secure from external attack. Its population was overwhelmingly rural and socially, politically, and economically conservative, with interests that were primarily local rather than national. China's ruling class, a relatively small bureaucratic elite, thoroughly dominated the country's sources of wealth and power. Members of the elite tended to pursue sociopolitical, scholarly, and artistic interests rather than military or commercial ones. China's traditional governmental and social structure functioned effectively most of the time, and left little room for the development of independent centers of power that might have challenged that structure. All of these factors, taken together, meant that China was on the one hand a rich and dynamic society that encouraged technological invention, and on the other hand an extremely stable society that was able to absorb innovation rather than be transformed by it.

Social Mobility and Social Stability

In premodern China the social pyramid consisted of the ruler and his family, a small ruling class, relatively small numbers of artisans and merchants, and a huge number of peasants. At the dawn of Chinese civilization, the ruling class was an aristocracy, holding power by right of birth. The aristocrats owned the land, controlled military power, and held government office. Around the time of Confucius, however—that is, around 500 B.C.—some members of the lowest level of the aristocracy began to rely on their literacy rather than their hereditary positions to advance their careers. Training themselves as writers, thinkers, and experts in history, they became free-lance political advisors to members of the higher aristocracy, and thus broke out of their low-level positions in the feudal hierarchy. Confucius himself stressed that merit was more important than birth in deciding who should hold government office. By the Han Dynasty, this principle was so thoroughly accepted that formal, competitive examinations were held regularly to choose new civil servants. Thus the Chinese institution of bureaucratic government was born.

Two young Chinese scholars in their library. From an album of papercut pictures, *ca.* 1955, done in the style of the late Ming Dynasty.

Of course, the aristocracy did not disappear overnight. For many more centuries members of the nobility played an important role in Chinese government, especially in the top ranks of the national administration. But one of the most important long-term trends in Chinese history was the replacement of aristocratic power by bureaucratic power. As time went on, members of the government were less and less likely to belong to ancient "great families," and more and more likely to have risen through the ranks of the civil service.

Members of the bureaucratic elite thoroughly dominated (although they did not quite monopolize) education, wealth, prestige, and power in traditional China. But, very importantly, they maintained that power only as long as, generation after generation, members of the family were able to pass the strict civil service examinations. This meant that families continually dropped out of the ruling class through laziness or misfortune, while the ruling class was continually enriched by vigorous new individuals rising from the lower classes. Individual bureaucrats might come and go; the bureaucracy as an institution and as a class lived on from dynasty to dynasty.

Membership in the ruling elite was by far the most desirable position in Chinese society, and it was at least potentially open to all. With few exceptions, all males were eligible to take the civil service examinations; success brought elite status not only to the man himself, but to his entire family. This single standard of success in Chinese society tended to work against the development of, for example, a commercial middle class; merchants, rich farmers, military officers, all wanted their sons to become bureaucrats.

The last vestiges of real aristocratic power in China vanished in the wars of dynastic succession that followed the fall of the Tang Dynasty in 907. The nonaristocratic character of the ruling class from the Song Dynasty onward gradually led to increasingly despotic rule on the part of China's emperors. Individual bureaucrats, totally dependent on the government for their power and prestige, protected themselves by being cautious and conformist. Unchallenged from within, and unchecked by alternative power centers in the aristocracy, the military, or the merchant class, China's imperial government tended to become increasingly centralized, more ponderous, and more stagnant. As the last dynasty, the Qing, came to an end, China was open to revolutionary social and political change that would sweep away the weight of its tired old government.

An Examination Question

By the end of the Qing Dynasty, the system of choosing officials by competitive examinations had existed in China for 2000 years. With the winds of republican revolution stirring in the early twentieth century, the last session of the palace examination (for candidates who had already passed the provincial examination) was held in 1903. One of the questions was the following:

How to create wealth is a subject commended by the Book of Great Learning. *Accordingly, consider the financial management of the past ages and submit for adoption any method that would benefit the government without harming the people.*

Part of one candidate's answer reads as follows:

In my humble opinion, if we wish to be powerful in the present circumstances we must first achieve wealth, and it is indeed the most urgent business before us. However, those in charge of finance only succeed in taxing, by various means, the existing wealth and possesssions of the people, in order to provide for the country's immediate expenditures. . . . It is unfortunately not realized that when something new is produced, the people will be benefitted by the addition, and the Universe will have more goods in circulation. When the people have enough, how can the ruler be inadequately supplied? This is fundamental to good government.

Adapted from T. C. Lai, *A Scholar in Imperial China: The Making of a Mandarin.* Hong Kong: Kelly & Walsh Ltd., 1970, pp. 49–50.

Social Disorder

The people of traditional China asked very little of their government by modern standards. They wanted military protection from external invasion and internal banditry; they did not want to be conscripted into the army too often or for too long. They wanted the government to maintain public works, such as roads and canals, and to avoid squandering money on huge palaces and royal tombs. They wanted the government to administer a system of justice, even though most civil cases and some criminal cases were settled privately, out of court. They wanted the government to maintain a supply of grain and other essential supplies to provide relief in case of natural disasters. Above all, they wanted tax rates to be kept as low as possible, and taxes to be collected honestly and fairly.

When a dynasty hit the down slope of the dynastic cycle, it began to be increasingly unable to meet these minimal expectations on the part of the people. Inattention to military preparedness and discipline left the country open to invasion and banditry. Corruption and extravagance meant the neglect of essential public works and the wasting of money on whims of the emperor and his family and friends. Inside the palace, lavish banquets were served on dishes of gold and jade; in the countryside, people starved. Favoritism and bribery corrupted the administration of justice. Above all, a dynasty in decline was a dynasty short of money, as influential citizens found ways to avoid paying their taxes. Stocks of emergency grain might then be sold, leaving the common people open to disaster when crops failed. Civil service examination degrees might be sold, demoralizing those bureaucrats who won their offices the hard way. Desperate to keep up its falling revenues, the government would raise tax rates; the burden fell on those too powerless to arrange tax exemptions. Small landowners often found that it was cheaper to pay rent than to pay taxes; they would sell their lands to a rich, tax-avoiding landlord and then rent them back again. But this only narrowed the tax base further, increasing the burden on those who still had to pay.

This was a recipe for trouble. Struggling peasants, pressed to the limit by rising taxes and faltering government, might be driven over the edge of despair by a flood, a famine, a drought, or the attacks of bandits. At that point they would rise in rebellion; their first acts would be to kill landlords and to attack the office of the local magistrate and burn the land-tax records. Most of the time, such local rebellions would be crushed quickly, and their leaders executed. Rarely, they would succeed in seizing local control from the government. As such scattered rebellions multiplied, and the government's ability to deal with them diminished, regional and even national rebel armies and leaders would arise, and the struggle to overthrow the old dynasty would begin. Eventually, a leader would claim the Mandate of Heaven, consolidate his power, and proclaim a new dynasty—one that, for a few generations at least, would once again satisfy the minimal expectations of the people.

This cycle of dynastic decline, maladministration, rising taxes, and rebellion was repeated dozens of times throughout Chinese history. It was a brutal and devastating, but effective, means of social and political renewal. In broad outline, it always followed the same basic pattern, and always had the same outcome; for centuries, no dynastic founder was able to devise a better model of government than the one he inherited from the past.

C H A P T E R   I V

Ancient China and the Early Imperial Period

The earliest ancestors of the Chinese people are lost in the depths of time. Early hominids ("Peking Man") lived in China several hundred thousand years ago, but scientists now believe that they died out without leaving direct descendants. True humans (the modern species *Homo sapiens*) probably migrated to China from western Asia sometime during the last Ice Age; stone tools used by ancient groups of hunter-gatherers dating to around 15,000 years ago have been found in scattered sites in both North and South China.

Around seven or eight thousand years ago, some of these people began to make the transition to an agricultural way of life—a transition known as the Neolithic Revolution. The Neolithic Period (the "new stone age") began when people depended more on cultivated plants for their food than on what they could find by hunting and gathering. Agriculture developed gradually. It began with the selective encouragement of fields of wild grasses (millet in the north, rice in the south) that yielded edible seeds, as well as by weeding patches of wild vegetables. Gradually this led to the selection and planting of seeds, and to harvesting and storing the resulting grain. Agriculture led to truly revolutionary changes in the way of life of these people. It meant living in one place rather than wandering in search of food, because fields had to be tended, and large harvests of grain were too bulky to carry. Hunter-gatherers have few possessions, because they need mobility. Farmers require tools, storage containers, a wider range of cooking utensils, and at least moderately sturdy houses and grain bins. Agriculture encourages the creation of villages, as people join together to share labor and resources, and to defend themselves and their fields against wild animals and other people. Most importantly, agriculture permits the creation of surplus wealth: things that are not needed for immediate daily life.

The Neolithic Revolution occurred in several parts of China, and differed in details from place to place. But in its broad outlines, the historical process was generally similar everywhere. Agriculture was accompanied by the domestication of animals (first dogs, pigs, and chickens, and later cattle and sheep), by an increasingly varied diet, and by larger and more permanent dwellings. Implements of stone, wood, bone, leather, and basketry were supplemented by pottery vessels, which grew steadily finer in workmanship and more diverse in shape and function. Production became specialized, as some people concentrated on the making of tools or pots and traded them to others for grain or other goods. Villages grew to become towns, and other types of specialists began to rely on food and goods produced by farmers and craftsmen; religious leaders, warriors, and administrators persuaded others to support them in return for the services that they provided.

In the northern grasslands, the agrarian Neolithic Revolution was paralleled by a pastoral revolution, as people learned the special skills associated with breeding animals and herding them on annual migrations. Nomads learned to ride horses instead of using them simply to pull wagons and chariots, and so gained extra speed and mobility for hunting, herding, and fighting. The northern frontier was already becoming significant. To the south, Neolithic cultures in the loess highlands and the North China Plain, in Liaoning and Shandong, in the Chang Jiang Valley and its delta, in Sichuan and Yunnan, and along the southeastern coast, were all ultimately to contribute to the formation of China's distinctive culture. As these centers of early settled culture developed over a period of thousands of years, however, one of them took the lead in shaping a distinctively Chinese culture. Chinese civilization has diverse roots, but its heartland was found in the Wei River and Yellow River valleys of north-central China.

Xia and Shang

The late Neolithic Period in northern China was described in Chinese mythology as a time of superhuman sage-kings who invented the essentials of civilization: agriculture, clothing and silk weaving, metalworking, writing, the calendar, and so on. Although such heroes as the Yellow Emperor probably never really existed, it is true that the late Neolithic reflects their supposed inventions. Beautifully made red pottery was painted with designs in black, including marks that seem to be the earliest forms of Chinese writing. Black pottery was made in shapes that later would be cast in bronze. Silkworms were cultivated and their cocoons unwound to weave cloth. Jade was carved into ornaments and ritual objects. The dead were buried with offerings, indicating a belief in an afterlife; religious specialists used special techniques to consult the spirits of the dead, showing that ancestor worship had already begun.

By around 2000 B.C., towns had grown into small cities on the North China Plain. Warrior-rulers, religious specialists, artisans, and farmers formed distinct social classes, and some were very much richer and more powerful than others.

One of these urban centers, near the present city of Zhengzhou, gave rise to the kingdom known as Xia. The proclamation of the Xia Kingdom may have coincided with an unusual clustering of the five visible planets in one small region of the sky in 1953 B.C. To the early Chinese, that gave visible proof that Heaven's approval had been given to the new royal house. (Of four such dense planetary groupings in the past 5000 years, three took place during the second millennium B.C., and each seems to have been associated with a change in the ruling dynasty of northern China.) We know little about the Xia kings. The dynastic founder was supposedly Yu the Great, a mythic hero who subdued a terrible flood that threatened the whole world. The kings were powerful enough, at least, to extend their political and military authority over part of the North China Plain, and to build impressive palaces and royal tombs.

China entered the Bronze Age during the Xia period. Historians argue about whether bronze was independently invented in China or whether the idea of making an alloy of copper and tin reached China from the older civilizations of the Middle East. In any case, the distinctive Chinese technique of casting bronze in ceramic molds was certainly developed locally. Bronze was used both for weapons and for implements used in religious rituals, such as sacrificial offerings of wine, grain, and meat. Few bronze vessels from the Xia period now survive, but they give a hint of the Xia Kingdom's wealth and power. Archaeological evidence also shows that the Xia rulers used a distinctively Chinese method of consulting the gods and royal ancestors by means of oracle bones. The shoulder bones of oxen or sheep, and the bottom shells of turtles, were cracked with a hot metal rod in a certain way and the shape of the cracks interpreted as a positive or negative answer to a question.

Heat-induced cracks in this turtle shell indicated the replies of the royal ancestors to questions asked by the Shang Dynasty kings. The principal historical records of the Shang are found on inscribed oracle bones like this one (reproduced as a rubbing for increased clarity). Note the difference between this archaic script and the later Chinese characters illustrated on p. 167. Photo courtesy of David Keightley, reproduced by permission of the Institute of History and Philology, Academia Sinica, Taipei, Taiwan, R.O.C.

The planetary conjunction of 1576 B.C. may have provided the occasion for the overthrow of the Xia by the founder of the Shang Dynasty, Tang the Victorious. The Shang continued the civilization of the Xia, extending the territory under its control and rising to new heights of wealth and power. Bronze casting was quickly raised to a level of technical and artistic sophistication that has never been surpassed. Wheat, goats, and the chariot reached China from the Middle East around 1300 B.C., providing new sources of agricultural wealth and military control. A military aristocracy emerged as a clearly defined ruling class that owed allegiance to the Shang kings. Palaces and tombs grew larger and more impressive. Shang kings and noblemen were buried with vast hoards of bronze vessels, implements of pottery and jade, and dozens of human and animal sacrifices. Kings sometimes went to war with neighboring peoples especially to obtain prisoners, who were killed and buried in tombs as servants for the dead. Excavations at the last Shang capital, near Anyang, have yielded thousands of artifacts from tombs, giving us a good picture of the life of the Shang ruling class.

The Shang people also left written records, the first in Chinese history. Questions for the gods and ancestors were inscribed on oracle bones, which were carefully stored in pits after they were used. The discovery of those bone archives in the early twentieth century brought Shang history out of the realm of legend and into concrete historical reality. The study of oracle bones continues to provide new information on the Shang nobility and ruling family, and on questions of religion, warfare, the economy, and much more.

The Zhou Dynasty

The neighbors of the Shang to the west, east, and south of the North

China Plain had also reached high levels of civilization, though without the central royal authority of the Shang. One of those neighbors, the state of Zhou in the Wei River Valley, rebelled against the misrule of the last Shang king; they pointed to the planetary conjunction of 1059 B.C. as a sign that Heaven's mandate had been given to them. The rule of the Zhou founders, kings Wen and Wu, was followed by that of the enlightened and capable Duke of Zhou, who served as regent for the infant third Zhou king. The speech of the Duke of Zhou to the defeated Shang nobility, asking them to submit to the will of Heaven, was preserved orally for several hundred years before it was written down, but it is probably an authentic record; it gives a vivid picture of royal authority and political theory in the China of 3000 years ago.

The Duke of Zhou extended the territory under his control far beyond the boundaries of the Shang state, by creating a genuine feudal system of rule. Clansmen and close allies of the Zhou royal family were made rulers of kingdoms throughout northern and central China. One Shang royal kinsman was kept alive and made ruler of a small state so that he could continue the sacrifices to the Shang royal ancestors, thus avoiding their angry retribution. The rulers had complete charge of the administration of their own kingdoms, and the collection of taxes within them; but they were pledged to attend the court of the Zhou king whenever they were summoned to do so, and to provide the Zhou kings with military support whenever necessary. Within their own states, the feudal lords were assisted by minor aristocrats, with their own estates, privileges, and military power. The Zhou state itself was under direct royal control, with its capital at Chang'an, on the banks of the Wei River—the first of several times that China's capital would be located there.

The Western Zhou, as the first period of the Zhou Dynasty is called, was in many ways a continuation of Shang civilization. There were, however, some noticeable differences. Bronze culture spread widely

The Mandate of Heaven

A few years after the Zhou overthrew the Shang (also called the Yin) Dynasty, the surviving members of the Shang aristocracy were deported to a newly built city called Lo. There they were called together and addressed by the Duke of Zhou, regent for the third Zhou king:

The king has spoken thus: You, the many surviving officers of Yin! The merciless and severe Heaven has sent down great destruction on Yin. We the Zhou have assisted the decree, and upholding Heaven's bright majesty we carried out the royal punishment and set aside Yin's mandate, which had been terminated by God. Now, all you officers, it was not that our small state dared to aspire to Yin's mandate. But Heaven's not giving favor to Yin was clear; it is not that we took advantage of Yin's disorder, but that Heaven helped us. . . .

I tell you this. You have been greatly lawless. I did not cause you to be deported here; the cause lies in your own city [i.e. the former Shang capital]. I also think of how Heaven has already greatly punished Yin, and so I do not punish you further. . . . I have not killed you, but I repeat to you my orders: What you, the many Yin officers, should do, is hasten to serve the Zhou with strict obedience. . . .

This speech (much shortened here) is the earliest statement in Chinese literature of the theory of the Mandate of Heaven.

Adapted from a translation by Bernhard Karlgren, *The Book of Documents* (Stockholm: Bulletin of the Museum of Far Eastern Antiquities, vol. 22, 1950), pp. 55–56.

throughout the area under Zhou control, but the shapes and decoration of vessels changed. Royal tombs became somewhat less extravagant (and burials less bloodthirsty), but military expenditures increased. The Zhou aristocracy gradually abandoned oracle bones, consulting their gods and ancestors instead by means of the *Book of Changes*, a fortune-telling manual still in use by many Chinese today. (It also has had some popularity in Europe and America.) Many written records exist from the Zhou period, both in the form of inscriptions cast into bronze vessels and in later editions of the first real Chinese books—collections of historical records, legends and songs, and royal documents. The courts of the feudal states fostered the development of an elaborate culture of protocol and diplomacy, ceremonial music and dance, religious rites, and literature and art. For ordinary people, of course, life was much less pleasant. Peasants and craftsmen were heavily taxed and were prohibited from migrating to other states; adult men were forced to perform labor and military service for the rulers. Women had to raise silkworms and weave silk cloth; part of their output went to the state treasury.

The Zhou feudal system worked well for its first two centuries or so, but then gradually began to break down. Rulers of the larger feudal states felt increasingly free to ignore the commands of the Zhou kings and act as independent powers. Larger states conquered and swallowed up smaller ones. In 781 B.C. the expanding state of Qin drove the Zhou kings from their capital and forced them to move to a much smaller territory along the Yellow River, with a new capital at Luoyang. The *Spring and Autumn Annals*, a chronicle kept by the dukes of the state of Lu from 722 to 481 B.C., tells of the decline of royal power during this Eastern Zhou period. For several generations, the rulers of the six largest states tried to fill the vacuum of authority by acting as "first among equals" within the feudal aristocracy. But they were unable to turn the tide of an age of constant danger and warfare, when alliances were constantly made and broken among the feudal states. The use of iron for tools and weapons, from the sixth century B.C. onward, gave further advantages to large, rich states and made the situation of small, weak ones more precarious. In Shang and early Zhou times, wars were fought by chariot-mounted aristocrats supported by peasant foot soldiers, and were restrained by a code of chivalrous conduct; by the middle Zhou, war was a winner-take-all affair fought by massive, well-armed infantry divisions. The administrative techniques of organizing large armies were also used to bring civilian populations under tighter government control. Many members of the old high aristocracy were driven from their thrones by their former ministers and generals, who razed the old ancestral shrines, abandoned all pretense of feudal hierarchy, and ruled their states as independent kings.

The division of the large, powerful state of Jin into three independent parts in 403 B.C. marked the beginning of the Warring States Period, a two-hundred-year struggle for survival. Philosophers and political advisors tried to find ways of restoring some kind of order within the collapsed Zhou system; generals and military advisors forged military alliances and tried out new strategies of war. Despite this, and despite a perception at the time that the world had degenerated into near anarchy, culture flourished. Both written records and archaeological evidence paint a picture of rich artistic, intellectual, and literary life. Aristocrats continued to be buried with treasure troves of bronze and jade. Commerce also flourished, and fortunes were made by dealers in grain, bronze, iron, salt, lacquer, and other goods. Advances in architecture, civil engineering (such as the building of irrigation systems and fortifications), and every field of craftsmanship point to the continued development of technology, as well as to the ability of rulers to mobilize money and manpower. Above all, the Warring States Period is known as the golden age of Chinese philosophy; Confucius is only the most famous of the many great thinkers who lived at this time (see Chapter VII).

Mass-produced Crossbows

Americans like to give credit to Sam Colt for inventing weapons with mass-produced, interchangeable parts. The Chinese, however, used exactly the same technique, beginning around 400 B.C., to produce bronze firing assemblies for crossbows. The simple but highly efficient mechanism consisted of three moving parts connected by two pins. Troops armed with crossbows fought the wars that led to China's unification under the Qin Dynasty in 221 B.C. The crossbow also provided the heavy firepower that the Chinese needed to defeat the fast, lightly-armed mounted nomad warriors of the northern frontier.

1. Trigger
2. Combined rear sight and bowstring holder
3. Lock
4. Bowstring
5. Arrow
6. Assembly pins

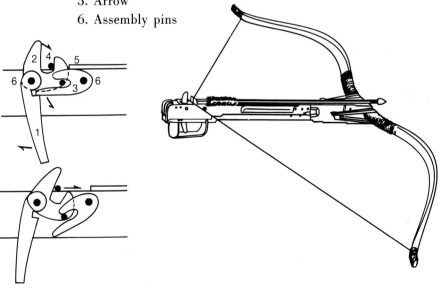

The Qin Unification

The last Zhou king died in 256 B.C., and his dynasty came to an end. The rulers of the handful of surviving feudal states fought to wipe each other out over the next thirty-five years, each seeking to reunify China under his own new dynasty. In a series of massive campaigns, the vigorous and capable young king of the state of Qin, in the Wei River Valley, overthrew his remaining rivals, most importantly the states of Qi in the northeast and Chu in the Chang Jiang Valley. The king of Qin had embraced a harsh new political philosophy known as legalism, under which all resources of the state were concentrated on military power; bravery on the battlefield was rewarded, offices were awarded on the basis of merit (especially military merit) rather than birth, and any resistance to the authority of the state was met with instant punishment. With his final military triumph in 221 B.C., the king of Qin proclaimed himself Shi Huangdi, the First Emperor, founder of a dynasty that was intended to last for a thousand generations. The First Emperor was a genuine unifier; one of his first acts was to institute standard, uniform currency and weights and measures throughout the empire.

The First Emperor overestimated the duration of his dynasty by 998 generations. The Qin Dynasty barely outlived its founder, and fell in 206 B.C. The policies that had created its devastating military power were less suited to peacetime rule and provoked bitter popular resentment. A contemporary critic was exaggerating when he said that punishments were so severe that there were whole counties where it was hard to find a man who had not had a foot or a hand chopped off, but he certainly captured the feelings of his time. The emperor spent vast sums building the Great Wall and preparing his own royal tomb, with its world-famous underground clay army; those projects subjected his people to heavy taxes and long periods of forced labor. A campaign in 213 B.C. to confiscate and burn all books in private hands (so that all knowledge would belong to the state), and to bury alive a number of scholars who were regarded as subversive, understandably alienated the literate elite. The emperor became mentally unstable; he spent less and less time on problems of government, but instead consulted with magicians and alchemists about how he might become physically immortal.

The First Emperor died in 210 B.C., and his son's elevation to the throne led to a period of intrigue, treachery, and murder within the palace, and rebellion and civil war throughout the country at large. Rebel armies sorted themselves out through battles and alliances, until by 206 B.C., there were only two serious rivals for the throne: Liu Bang, from the former small northern state of Han, and Xiang Yu, from the former state of Chu. The issue between them was not simply a quest for personal power, but also a test between the two great regional variants of early Chinese civilization, those of the North China Plain and the Chang Jiang Valley. Liu Bang's victory—he proclaimed the founding of the Han Dynasty in 206 B.C., and consolidated his rule over the next four years—ensured that the center of political power in China would remain in the north, despite the growing economic power and cultural influence of the south.

The Han Empire

Liu Bang (later known as Han Gaozu, the High Ancestor of Han) abolished the Qin legalist system and, imitating the Duke of Zhou, reinstituted a feudal system. He appointed his relatives and loyal supporters as kings of large states, expanding the boundaries of the empire in the process; but he was careful to ensure that overwhelming power remained in his own hands. Nevertheless, the tide of Chinese history was running in favor of bureaucracy over aristocracy, and centralism over feudalism. During the next eighty years, the founder's successors drove the regional kings into retirement, executed them, or forced them to commit suicide. The reabsorbed territories were divided into provinces and counties under the control of appointed officials, who soon came to be selected either through recommendations to the throne or by competitive examinations. Following the path that had been prepared by the brief but influential Qin Dynasty, the Han created a style of imperial bureaucratic government that, in its basic outlines, was to endure for over two thousand years.

The first half of the Han period (the Former Han, or Western Han, with its capital again at Chang'an) was one of the greatest eras in Chinese history. Under Emperor Wu (140–87 B.C.), the Han decisively defeated the Xiongnu nomads of the north, setting off a shock wave of "barbarian" migrations westward that ultimately would lead, centuries later, to the Hun invasions of Rome. The result of that victory was that China controlled the northern frontier and the Gansu Corridor, opening up the Silk Route to regular annual trade between China and Syria; fine horses from Central Asia strengthened the imperial armies. Emperor Wu established Chinese colonies in northern Korea, brought Yunnan and the coastal regions of southeastern China into the empire, and encouraged the growth of maritime commerce (although still on a small scale) in the South China Sea. Although Emperor Wu fought wars of expansion, internally the empire was at peace, and the dynasty enjoyed both elite and popular support. The decline of feudalism paved the way for the private ownership of land, which led to an expansion of land under cultivation, the construction of new terraces and irrigation and drainage systems, and improved agricultural productivity. This, in turn, led to an increase in the population, an increase not depleted by constant warfare as in earlier times. (During the Han, the population of

China was about 50 million, still small in relation to available resources; more people were an advantage rather than a burden.)

The unified empire with its focus on the imperial capital led to the integration into mainstream Chinese culture of a variety of regional cultural styles. Lacquer and silk brocade from the Chang Jiang Valley, gem coral from the southeastern coast, jade from the far northwest, and furs from the northeast, all were traded throughout the empire; the exchange of ideas, beliefs, and artistic styles was equally widespread. Poets wrote of the brilliance and luxury of the imperial court; masters of ceremonial created new rituals for the emperors to display their power and authority. Aristocrats complained that merchants were exceeding their rank, growing even more wealthy than the nobility. Craftsmen prospered; even peasants were reasonably well off, and some moved to new, unsettled territories to improve their fortunes. Intellectual life flourished; philosophers created a new official ideology composed of Confucian ethics, administrative theory, and astrology, on which candidates for office were examined at court. The court historian Sima Qian wrote the *Records of the Historian*, the first of China's massive official histories.

By the end of the first century B.C., the Han Dynasty was troubled by factionalism at court, and a succession of weak emperors. A high minister, Wang Mang, seized power in A.D. 7, and tried to establish a new dynasty of his own. He was briefly successful, but his rule was undermined by unpopular policies and natural disasters. The Liu clan, aided by most of the aristocracy, rose again to reestablish the Han, with a new capital in the east at Luoyang. The Latter Han, or Eastern Han, period lasted for two centuries, but never recaptured the brilliance of the first half of the Han Dynasty. New groups of nomads raided the northern frontier, the Korean colonies were abandoned, and trade on the Silk Route declined. The last fifty years of the Latter Han were marked by intrigue at court, a loss of confidence within the bureaucratic

The Travels of Zhang Qian

When Emperor Wu of the Han Dynasty came to the throne in 140 B.C., the Chinese had been at war for decades with the Xiongnu, the dominant nomadic tribe in what is now Mongolia. The Xiongnu had recently defeated a rival tribe, the Yuezhi, who had then migrated from their base in northwestern Gansu Province all the way to Bactria, along the banks of the Oxus (Amu Darya) River, near the present-day city of Bukhara in Soviet Uzbekistan. Emperor Wu devised a plan to form an alliance with the Yuezhi against the Xiongnu, and asked for a volunteer to undertake the hazardous journey to the far west. A palace official named Zhang Qian answered the call.

Zhang's route to the new homeland of the Yuezhi took him through Xiongnu territory, and he was promptly captured. He was held prisoner for ten years, and although he was treated kindly (he was given a Xiongnu wife for companionship), he never forgot his imperial orders. At last he escaped; making his way through the Tarim Basin and Ferghana (near Tashkent), he arrived in Bactria in

elite, and the rise of new, salvation-oriented popular religions that provided the focus for massive peasant rebellions. The dynasty collapsed in disarray in 220 A.D. The empire was divided into three competing kingdoms: Shu in Sichuan, ruled by a remnant of the Han imperial house; Wei in the North China Plain; and Wu in the Chang Jiang Valley. The two greatest generals of the time, Zhuge Liang of Shu and Cao Cao of Wei, are known to every Chinese today as the hero and the villain of dozens of stories and operas.

128 B.C. He found that the king of the Yuezhi had no desire to resume the old war with the Xiongnu, but that he—like other Central Asian rulers—was very much interested in opening up diplomatic and trade relations with China.

On his journey home, Zhang Qian was again captured by the Xiongnu; escaping after a year, he arrived in Chang'an to receive his richly deserved reward. His detailed reports about the lands he had visited and others he had heard about (including India) inspired Emperor Wu to pursue a policy of bringing all of Central Asia under Chinese domination. More embassies were sent westward. The Western Horde of the Xiongnu was decisively defeated in 121 B.C. In 100 B.C. a 60,000-man Chinese army crossed the Tarim Basin to force the king of Ferghana to submit to Chinese domination.

Thus within twenty-eight years of Zhang Qian's mission to the Yuezhi, a network of Chinese military conquest and diplomacy extended almost as far west as the Caspian Sea. The Silk Route was brought firmly under Chinese control. The annual caravans bringing silk to Persia and Syria would also, in centuries to come, carry a steady stream of ideas and techniques between China and the West.

The Period of Disunion

Although the Three Kingdoms Period (A.D. 220–263) is remembered today as an almost legendary era of romance and chivalry, in fact it marked the end of China's first great imperial era. When Shu, Wei, and Wu fell apart in the 260s, China entered a period of over three centuries of disunion. The empire was split fundamentally between north and south, and within each region a series of short-lived dynasties tried without success to put the empire back together again. The north was relatively more stable; the Jin Dynasty controlled parts of the north from 263 to 420, and the Wei Dynasty ruled, also in parts of the north, from 386 to 534. But both suffered from uncertain boundaries and shifting capitals; the Wei moreover was a foreign dynasty, founded by the Toba nomads of the far northeast. South China was politically fragmented throughout the Period of Disunion.

Han Confucianism declined along with the imperial system it was designed to support. China's literate elite turned their attention instead toward two new systems of belief: Buddhism and Daoism. Buddhism arrived in China from Central Asia sometime during the Latter Han period; its world-denying creed proved very appealing in an age of increasing instability. Actively patronized by China's rulers, especially under the Wei Dynasty, Buddhist monasteries grew rich and powerful; the piety of rich and poor believers alike helped to create beautiful temples and grottos containing some of the finest sculpture ever produced in China. The Daoist religion developed toward the end of the Latter Han, from roots in earlier Daoist philosophy as well as diverse popular religious cults. It, too, prospered during the Period of Disunion. Intellectuals throughout China often devoted themselves to the study of scriptures in preference to careers as bureaucrats. Among the best-known writers of the time were the Seven Sages of the Bamboo Grove, known as much for their aversion to public office and their eccentric behavior as for their essays and poetry. The poet Tao Qian breathed a sigh of relief—"Too long have I been caught in the dusty net"—when he retired from office to pursue a quiet literary life on his farm.

Sui and Tang

The Period of Disunion came to an end in 589, when the founder of the Sui Dynasty reunited the empire through a combination of military

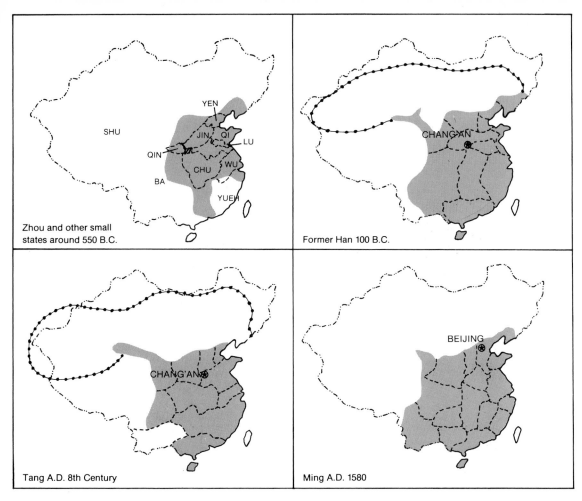

Zhou and other small states around 550 B.C.

YEN
JIN QI
LU
QIN
CHU WU
BA
SHU
YUEH

Former Han 100 B.C.

CHANG'AN

Tang A.D. 8th Century

CHANG'AN

Ming A.D. 1580

BEIJING

⊛ locations of imperial capitals as named
•••• frontier zones of Chinese political influence
–·–· greater China as of about 1890
▨ surviving Zhou royal domain
▨ area under control of the Chinese state

Historical Maps:
550 B.C.; 100 B.C.; A.D. 700; A.D. 1580

force and skillful diplomacy. In many ways, the Sui Dynasty resembles the Qin Dynasty of China's first emperor. It unified the empire after a long period of disunion; it attempted to do too much too quickly; it did not endure long, but it paved the way for a great and powerful dynasty to follow. The second Sui emperor is best known for having built the Grand Canal, which linked the Chang Jiang delta to the capital at

Chang'an. That was a great achievement, allowing rice from the rich southlands to be brought by barge to the north; but the cost in taxes and manpower of building the canal was very high. The same emperor spent still more money at the same time in a disastrous, unsuccessful attempt to conquer Korea. He was strongly criticized by the still-powerful northern aristocracy for preferring to spend too much of his time in the luxurious south. In 617 a new military leader from the northwest, Li Shimin, joined his father in rebellion against the Sui; in the following year, they founded the Tang Dynasty.

The Tang empire quickly equaled and then surpassed the glory of the Han Dynasty. A string of military garrisons along the Silk Route pushed Chinese power farther into Central Asia than ever before; trade flourished, leading to the creation of new wealth and an exchange of goods, ideas, techniques, and artistic influence between China and Persia. (For example, under Persian or Turkish influence the Chinese began to sit on chairs rather than on mats or cushions on the floor. New types of musical instruments were also imported from western Asia.) A marriage alliance brought Tibet into China's political orbit; in the south, the boundaries of the empire were extended into northern Vietnam. Chinese Buddhist pilgrims traveled to India, both overland and by sea. Embassies from Japan and Korea helped to make Chinese culture dominant in both of those countries. The Tang capital at Chang'an was the largest, wealthiest, and most cosmopolitan city in the world. Its population approached one million, and included resident communities of people from as far away as Syria, Armenia, Korea, and Malaya. Splendid

The Grand Canal, Suzhou. Built in the early seventh century A.D. to transport rice from the Chang Jiang delta to the North China Plain, the canal remains an important transportation artery today. Long strings of barges pulled by tugboats provide a slow but inexpensive means of moving freight.

palaces and imperial parks graced the capital, paid for by taxes of rice and silk transported northward on the Grand Canal.

For its first century and a half, the Tang empire was huge, internally at peace, and blessed with a large but not overwhelming population. Even with moderate tax rates, the empire generated vast amounts of wealth, which supported a brilliant cultural life. Wealthy people in fine mansions ate from plates of the newly developed three-colored glazed pottery and drank from cups of silver, gold, or jade; they dressed in silk robes cut in ever-changing fashions. Officials chosen by written examinations staffed a well-organized and efficient government. The arts flourished; every upper-class gentleman was expected to be a poet, a painter, a musician, and a connoisseur of art. Scholarship in all of the three teachings—Buddhism, Daoism, and a revived Confucianism—thrived, and the government established imperial academies to support the finest writers, historians, religious scholars, and scientists. Upperclass women often were well educated and enjoyed more personal independence than ever before.

The Tang Dynasty is remembered particularly for its poetry. Three of the greatest poets in Chinese history lived in the mid-eighth century; they witnessed the height of Tang power, but also its decline. The brilliant Li Bo, whose drunken brawling was excused because of his poetic genius, wrote happily of moonlight parties of wine drinking and music. A few years later Du Fu, in retirement at his "thatched hut" in Chengdu, wrote of the sufferings of the common people as civil war tore the empire apart. A Tang general, An Lushan, attempted to seize power in 755, and war raged for eight years before the Tang emperor reclaimed the throne. The flight of the emperor from the capital during

A huge stone figure of an official guards the road leading to the tomb of the third emperor of the Tang Dynasty (died A.D. 683).

An Lushan's rebellion, and the death of the emperor's favorite concubine, Yang Guifei, were the subject of the most popularly beloved poem in all of Chinese literature, Bo Juyi's "Song of Unending Regret."

In 751, just before the rebellion, Chinese troops in Central Asia had been defeated at the Battle of Talas by Arab forces, the vanguard of Islamic expansion into what is now Afghanistan. Chinese control over the Silk Route collapsed. In 767, the governors of the four northern provinces rebelled and won the right to make their offices hereditary thereafter. The Tang Dynasty survived, but it was weakened both externally and internally. Political instability in the north set the stage for the subsequent permanent dominance of the south in China's economic and intellectual life. Throughout the country a crucial danger signal of dynastic weakness appeared: land tax rates were raised by the financially strapped government, while huge, tax-evading private estates grew ever larger.

Both Buddhism and Daoism flourished during the Tang; it was an age of both religious piety and great theological scholarship. In the latter half of the period, tens of thousands of people became monks, either to escape from a disordered world into a life of prayer or to evade taxes and military conscription—often, perhaps, both. But both religions began gradually to lose their appeal for the intellectual elite, as a revival of Confucianism began to take hold. At the end of the eighth century, the noted writer and scholar-official Han Yu denounced Buddhism as a "barbarian" religion unworthy of the emperor's attention. This appeal to Chinese chauvinism was a far cry from the cosmopolitan outlook of a century before. In the 840s, a mentally unstable emperor ordered a great purge of Buddhism, destroying many temples, melting down bronze sacred images, confiscating monastic estates, and defrocking (and returning to the tax roll) thousands of monks. (The policy made economic sense; its ferocity made no sense at all.)

The end of the Tang followed the familiar script of the dynastic cycle. Factionalism, corruption, and imperial inattention sapped the strength of the bureaucracy. Suffering peasants rose in rebellion as nomads raided the ill-defended northern frontier. A series of weak emperors seemed incapable of understanding, let alone halting, the process of dynastic disintegration. The once glorious Tang Dynasty fell to a rebel army in 907.

Over the next fifty years, five dynasties rose and fell, none able to secure its grip on the throne. The dynastic wars of that period dealt a death blow to China's old aristocracy; most of the great families of the Tang, especially in the north, had been exterminated or had fallen into obscurity by the middle of the tenth century. The Song Dynasty, which ascended the throne in 960, was to mark a transition to China's early modern era.

Medieval and Late Imperial China

The culture and society of traditional China are rooted in deep antiquity, but much of what seems most characteristic when we think of premodern China began to assume its familiar form during the Song Dynasty (960–1279). Landscape painting, fine porcelain, foot-binding, and landscaped gardens are all Song developments. The professional civil service, already an old institution by the Song, began to take on its fully developed character: nonaristocratic, broadly based within the upper reaches of Chinese society, motivated by an orthodox Confucian ideology, and selected on the basis of merit as demonstrated in competitive examinations. Printing and gunpowder, both invented during the Tang Dynasty (618–907), came into widespread use during the Song. For the first time China emerged as a major maritime power, leading to a significant expansion of overseas trade and to the establishment of communities of Chinese merchants in Southeast Asia. In all of these ways, the Song represents a transitional phase between ancient and early imperial China and the final stages of the imperial era.

Establishment of the Song Dynasty

The half century following the fall of the Tang Dynasty was a time of social instability, perennial warfare, political turmoil, and great suffering among the common people. When, in 959, the second emperor of the Later Zhou Dynasty (the last of the post-Tang Five Dynasties) died, Zhao Kuangyin—a high civil and military official from an important family—was appointed regent for the emperor's young son. In 960, Zhao Kuangyin proclaimed the founding of his own dynasty, the Song, and set about defeating his rivals among the military leaders and rulers of petty states in central and southern China. Within a decade, he had reconsolidated the empire under his rule, securing the position of a dynasty that would last for three hundred years.

The Song founder's achievement was not complete. During the Five Dynasties, much of northern China—including portions of the North China Plain well inside the Great Wall—had fallen under the control of the Khitan Mongols (whose name has given us the name Cathay). The Khitan leaders proclaimed themselves emperors of the Liao Dynasty, employing the Chinese elite in the territory under their control to run a Chinese-style bureaucratic state on their behalf. Despite a long and costly war, the Song were unable to dislodge the Liao, and recognized their control of the north in a treaty in 1005. The northwest, too, had been lost to Chinese rule; in 990 the Tangut Tibetan tribal confederation established the kingdom of Xixia in the Ordos Plateau and the

Gansu Corridor. The Song Dynasty, despite its cultural brilliance, ruled a very much smaller empire than its great predecessors the Han and the Tang.

Control of the north was to remain a perennial problem for the Song, and indeed was to be a persistent theme in the history of late imperial China. For seven hundred of the thousand years following the fall of the Tang, "barbarian" emperors ruled part or all of China. The Song achieved a measure of security only through the humiliating policy of paying huge annual "gifts" of money and trade goods to the rulers of the northern frontier. Although it could thus boast of little of the military glory of earlier ages, the Song, with its new capital at Kaifeng, consolidated its control over a large part of the Chinese heartland and set out to make the most of it.

With the passing of the old northern aristocracy, and the physical loss of territory in the north, China during the Song turned as never before to aspects of life dominated by civil (rather than military or political) values. The social, intellectual, and cultural life of the empire was dominated by the wealthy families of the Chang Jiang Valley. Education was more widely available than it had ever been before, spurred on by the increased circulation of printed books and the opening of private academies. The ruling class, turning away from Buddhism and Daoism, devoted itself to classical studies in the Confucian tradition; this was reflected both in the content of the civil service examinations and in the vigor of philosophy as an academic discipline. The arts flourished in an atmosphere of wealth and leisure. It was not unusual for even the highest officials to be also great artists: Ouyang Xiu and Sima Guang were both high ministers and also great prose writers; the greatest poet of the age, Su Shi, had a distinguished political career. The emperor Huizong (reigned 1101–1126) is still regarded as one of the finest painters and calligraphers of the time.

The wealth of the Song upper class was reflected in the general prosperity of the time. Luxury industries, such as silk weaving and porcelain making, found an endless demand for their products, as did architects and landscape designers. Rice production reached new heights. The merchant class—dealers in all of these products and many more—became more wealthy and prominent than ever before. Technology, from water clocks to agricultural machines to shipbuilding, gave rise to a great era of invention. Responding to a time of peace and prosperity, the population rapidly recovered from the devastation of the early tenth century; by 1100, the population of China (including areas under Liao and Xixia control) approached 125 million; at least five cities had populations of a million or more.

A political controversy set the stage for a near disaster in the middle of the Song Dynasty. The prime minister Wang Anshi (1021–1086), a great administrator but a difficult personality, proposed a series of sweeping reforms in the civil service examinations and the central government administration. His proposals had the effect of polarizing the bureaucracy into competing factions, pro-reform and anti-reform. The controversy continued after Wang's death, distracting the government from new danger in the north.

By the end of the eleventh century a group of tribal people in the Amur Valley known as the Jurchen (ancestors of the later Manchu conquerors of China) began to attack the northeastern frontiers of the Liao realm in the north. By 1115 they had swept away the Liao Dynasty and proclaimed their own Jin Dynasty; they then tried to conquer the Song as well. They almost succeeded. In 1126 they sacked Kaifeng, taking prisoner the emperor and 3000 high officials. A young cousin of the emperor escaped, however, fled south to Hangzhou, and reestablished the dynasty there in 1127, beginning a period known as the Southern Song. Hostilities continued until 1142; the Song resisted

A nomad chieftain returns home to the steppe with his bride, a Chinese princess. Detail from a fourteenth-century hand-scroll painting, Eighteen Songs of a Nomad Flute, *Metropolitan Museum of Art.*   Gift of the Dillon Fund, 1973 (1973.120.3).

conquest successfully, largely with the aid of gunpowder weapons and a superior navy. A truce was concluded, in which the Song court agreed to pay a large ransom to the Jin rulers of the north every year in return for peace.

With its economic base in the Chang Jiang Valley intact, the Southern Song quickly recovered its prosperity and stability. With its capital on the coast for the first time in history, the imperial court encouraged overseas trade and was far friendlier toward the merchant class than previous dynasties had been. Chinese mariners soon dominated the shipping lanes between China and India; the volume of trade was so great that Chinese copper coins became common currency all over Southeast Asia. Porcelain was exported as far afield as Zanzibar and the Persian Gulf. Scholarship flourished as well. Zhu Xi (1130–1200), one of the greatest philosophers in Chinese history, the author of the definitive works of Neo-Confucianism, lived during the height of the Southern Song. Astronomy, medicine, and mathematics all made great advances during the same period.

At the dawn of the thirteenth century, however, the forces that would sweep away the Song Dynasty were already gathering in the north. Genghis Khan, the greatest conquerer in history, was beginning to dream of ruling the world.

The Mongol Empire

Temujin, who was to become known as Genghis Khan (1167?–1227) was the son of a powerful Mongol leader. But at the age of fourteen, he found himself a penniless orphan, struggling simply to survive. Vowing revenge against those who had reduced him to that state, he attacked and defeated his enemies one by one, showing uncommon courage and ruthlessness even by the standards of a people that encouraged those qualities in everyone. Relentless against his enemies, winning allies by his success and the force of his personality, he headed a tribal confederation that controlled all of Mongolia by 1206. In 1205 he had moved against the Tangut Xixia kingdom in northwestern China, and four years later attacked the Jin Dynasty itself. He sacked the Jin capital at Beijing in 1215, and then turned his attention westward, leading a series of campaigns that brought most of Asia, all the way to the eastern shore of the Mediterranean, under Mongol control. He was killed in battle in 1227, in a campaign to put down a Tangut rebellion.

Genghis Khan's four sons continued their father's conquests, leading Mongol armies into the Ukraine, Russia, and Hungary. In the East they conquered Korea in 1231 and wiped out the remainder of the Jin Dynasty in 1234, giving them control over all of northern China. The Mongols were ruthless but intelligent conquerers. They would slaughter the population of any city that resisted conquest, but were generous toward those that submitted without a fight. In the last year of his life Genghis Khan had accepted the advice of Yelu Qucai—a descendant of the old Khitan Liao royal family—that taxation was a more reliable long-term source of wealth than plunder. This undoubtedly saved tens of millions of people from additional suffering. The Mongols were quick to use the resources of conquered peoples to aid in still further conquests. Chinese engineers fought with Mongol armies in Turkey; Alan warriors from the Caucasus were present at the siege of Kaifeng in 1234.

With the Mongol Empire spreading in the north, the Song emperors debated about what to do. Some advisers urged a continuation of the policy of tribute and appeasement that had worked with the Jurchens; others urged military action. The decision—a preemptive attack against the Mongols in North China in 1234—was a catastrophe that led only to Mongol determination to destroy the Song. Despite their historical reputation for military weakness, the Song resisted bloodily for forty-five years. Their rockets, bombs, and warships slowed the Mongols at the Huai River, until the Mongols themselves learned the techniques of gunpowder and naval warfare. The rice paddies, canals, and hot weather of the south were difficult and unfamiliar to Mongol horsemen, who were also weakened by strange new warm-climate diseases. Nevertheless, the last years of the Song were taken up by a sheer struggle for survival.

The Mongol Empire had been divided into three regions by the sons of Genghis Khan. In 1260 one of the conquerer's grandsons, Kubilai Khan, became emperor of the eastern region and promptly rebuilt Beijing to serve as his winter capital. By the time he crushed the last resistance of the Song in 1279, he had already set up an energetic and well-run Chinese-style administration in the north.

The Yuan Dynasty

Kubilai Khan inherited his grandfather's interest in conquest. Korea was used in 1274 and 1281 as the staging area for two invasions of Japan. In both cases the Mongol fleets were destroyed by typhoons (which the Japanese called *kamikaze*, "divine winds") after the invaders had gone ashore; the stranded troops were picked off by Japanese samurai armies. Mongol troops transported by Chinese warships conquered most of Vietnam, but were defeated when they tried to invade Java. After that, Kubilai Khan's enthusiasm for expanding his empire waned, and he devoted himself primarily to ruling China.

The Mongols, realizing that they were a tiny minority within the huge population of China, tried to reinforce their control through ethnic strength and purity enforced through regulations requiring Mongols and Chinese to use their own languages, dress, and customs, and prohibiting intermarriage. Mongol garrisons were stationed throughout the country (much to the resentment of the local Chinese population). Kubilai Khan preferred to use Mongol or foreign officials rather than Chinese ones; in any case, many former Song officials went into retirement rather than switch allegiance to their conquerers. The Italian merchant Marco Polo, who was in China from 1275 to 1292, served as one of the Khan's officials, although he never learned Chinese. Numerous Persian and Central Asian Moslem officials also staffed the Khan's bureaucracy and helped to spread Islam in China.

Though he ruled as a foreigner, Kubilai Khan ruled China well. He understood that land formed the basis of his country's wealth, and quickly repaired the ravages of war. Irrigation systems were rebuilt; a new branch of the Grand Canal linked Beijing with Hangzhou. Charity hospitals were constructed, and welfare relief was distributed to the poor. The Mongols were great patrons of science and technology

Paper Money

During his visit to China Marco Polo was astonished to see paper money being used in commercial transactions. In his *Travels*, he described this wonderful innovation in detail:

The Khan has money made for him by the following process, out of the bark of trees—to be precise, from mulberry trees. . . . The fine layer between the bark and the wood of the tree is stripped off. Then it is crumbled and pounded and flattened out with the aid of glue into sheets . . . which are cut up into rectangles of various sizes. . . . And all these papers are sealed with the seal of the Great Khan. The procedure of issue is as formal and as authoritative as if they were made of pure gold or silver. On each piece of money several specially appointed officials write their names, and affix their stamps. When it is completed in due form, the chief of the officials assigned by the Khan dips in cinnabar ink the seal assigned to him and stamps it on top of the piece of money so that the shape of the seal remains impressed on it in vermilion. And then the money is authentic. If anyone were to counterfeit it, he would suffer the extreme penalty.

Adapted from the translation by R.E. Latham, *Marco Polo: The Travels* (Hammondsworth, England: Penguin, 1958), p. 147. Reproduced by permission of Penguin Books Ltd.

throughout their empire; in the 1270s Kubilai Khan employed the Chinese astronomer Guo Shoujing to build the world's best observatory in Beijing.

Under the Yuan Dynasty, China was for the first time part of an integrated Eurasian international community. The "Pax Mongolica" (Mongol Peace) made travel and trade safe and relatively convenient from Korea to the Danube. There were resident communities in Beijing of merchants from Russia and Constantinople; a Chinese Nestorian Christian ambassador of Kubilai Khan met King Philip the Fair in Paris. Inspired by Islamic tilework and the availability of high-quality cobalt from Persia, Chinese potters began to manufacture blue-and-white porcelain. Chinese landscape painting had a deep influence on the development of Persian miniature painting. The Mongols' complete toleration of all religions led to the spread of Lamaism, the Tibetan form of Buddhism, to Mongolia and China, and facilitated the eastward expansion of Islam. People, ideas, and merchandise moved freely in all directions. (So did germs: During the Mongol Period an outbreak of plague in Afghanistan spread to both Europe and China, causing millions of deaths.)

All was not well with the Mongol government of China, however. Following the death of Kubilai Khan's son Timur in 1308, Chinese resentment of "barbarian" rule gradually developed into outright rebellion. The Mongols' failure to make full use of traditional Chinese bureaucratic government, and their preference for employing foreigners as senior officials, led to deep dissatisfaction within China's upper class of scholar-officials. After two generations of peace, the Mongol garrisons were viewed by officials and commoners alike as expensive, arrogant, and useless occupying armies. Although Chinese culture—particularly painting, drama, and the decorative arts—flourished during the Yuan period, many Chinese felt increasingly oppressed by the foreignness of their rulers. It was time, many felt, to see a Chinese emperor on the dragon throne once again.

In the atmosphere of rebellion that marked China in the mid-fourteenth century, a charismatic Buddhist monk, Zhu Yuanzhang, began to preach a religious message aimed at Chinese nativist feelings. When one of his rallies in Shandong Province was broken up by Mongol troops, a riot ensued. Zhu soon found himself at the head of a tide of rebellion. He was well suited to the task. Both intelligent and cruel, he wiped out any other rebel leaders whom he could not win to his own cause; toning down the religious content of his message, he was able to enlist the support of disgruntled Confucian intellectuals.

Zhu Yuanzhang's army captured Nanjing in 1356, and drove the Mongols out of Beijing twelve years later. Amidst the ruins of the Mongol Forbidden City, he proclaimed himself founder of the Ming Dynasty. The breakup of the Mongol Empire had begun. China was once again in Chinese hands, and the Ming empire soon controlled almost as much territory as the Tang Dynasty at its height.

The Ming Dynasty

Zhu Yuanzhang established his dynastic capital at Nanjing, and devoted himself to the reestablishment of Confucian bureaucratic government and to restoring the war-ravaged countryside. In his later years, how-ever, he became somewhat irrational, and his cruel streak dominated his personality. Whole clans of high officials were slaughtered on his orders for largely imaginary acts of disloyalty, spreading fear and suspi-cion throughout the ruling class. His death in 1399 was greeted with relief. He had named his grandson as his successor and heir; one of his sons, resentful of this, rose in rebellion in the north. The entire country, having just recovered from the rebellion against the Mongols, was plunged into civil war. By 1403 the son had driven his nephew from the throne and established his own capital at Beijing. Taking the title of the Yongle (Eternal Felicity) Emperor of Ming, he ushered in one of the most brilliant reigns in Chinese history.

The new emperor was mindful of his father's advice about keeping the bureaucracy under control, but he also actively courted the support of the scholar-official class. His administration was more centralized and authoritarian than that of the Song emperors (and in this, he set a pattern for the future), but he also cultivated an image of himself as a patron of learning and the arts. The Yongle Compendium, a beautifully produced collection of classical literature in 11,000 volumes, was an enduring monument to Ming scholarship.

The Yongle Emperor's dominant interest, however, was foreign relations. Motivated in part by memories of Mongol internationalism, he set out to make China the center of all of Asia. In this, his successes outweighed his failures. He fought off Timur Leng in Central Asia and the Oirat Mongols in the north—defeating the last gasps of Mongol empire building. In Korea he cultivated the support of the new Yi Dynasty (which had replaced the pro-Mongol Koryŏ Dynasty in 1392); Korea thereafter was the most fervent foreign ally of the Ming. On the other hand, Tibet, under King Songtsan Gampo, broke away from the Chinese empire, as did Vietnam. (Chinese ambitions in both places would persist long into the future.)

Like the Portuguese Prince Henry the Navigator a generation later, the Yongle Emperor was a great patron of maritime exploration. In a series of voyages between 1405 and 1433, Grand Admiral Zheng He sailed the largest ships the world had ever seen to the East Indies, India, Sri Lanka, the Persian Gulf, the Red Sea, and the east coast of Africa as far south as the Cape of Good Hope. These voyages greatly increased China's knowledge of the rest of the world, spread the prestige of the Ming Dynasty far and wide, fostered overseas trade, and even brought a giraffe back to Beijing for the imperial zoo. They also, unfortunately for China, were only a brief flash of glory that was followed by China's abrupt decline as an international power.

The Yongle Emperor's successors, under the influence of conservative Confucian advisors, regarded maritime exploration and trade as a useless extravagance. By the 1440s, the imperial shipyards were abandoned, and even private citizens were prohibited from venturing overseas. (Some merchants ignored this law, and continued to trade with Southeast Asia.) The coast was left undefended, open to raids by Japanese pirates. On the inland frontiers, too, military defense was replaced by a policy of appeasement. Rulers of nearby countries were encouraged to send embassies bringing what the emperors liked to think of as "tribute" to the imperial court; they returned home with "gifts" of far greater value. In fact, this so-called tribute system worked in many cases as a prettied-up method of bribing "barbarians" to maintain peace on China's frontiers. At the worst possible historical moment, China turned inward, shrinking from contact with the rest of the world.

In 1497–1498, Vasco Da Gama sailed from Portugal around Africa to India; at the same time, Columbus was showing the world how the circle might be completed from the other direction. By the early sixteenth century Portuguese mariners were regularly sailing in the South China Sea; in 1557 they asked for and got permission from China to establish a small colony at Macao, near Guangzhou in the Pearl River Delta. The Portuguese, and later the Spanish, Dutch, and English, came to China to trade, not (as in much of the rest of the world) to conquer. Yet the Ming, and their successors the Qing, looking inward, remained unaware of the extent of European expansion in southern Asia. By the time the Chinese realized that they themselves were threatened, it was too late to do anything about it.

Because of the weakness of its foreign policy after the mid-fifteenth century, the Ming Dynasty has had a rather bad historical reputation. Nevertheless, it was also a time of prosperity, internal peace, and cultural attainment. Although members of the scholar-official class had less room for independence of thought than their predecessors during the Song period, they were prosperous and generally contented. The population grew to about 250 million people, reflecting a highly developed agricultural economy, a well-ordered society, and generally successful government attempts to cope with occasional natural disasters. During the sixteenth century new food crops—including peanuts, sugar cane, sweet potatoes, and corn—enriched the Chinese diet. All the arts flourished; particularly notable was the development of a new genre of literature, prose fiction.

By 1600, however, the Ming had clearly reached the stage of dynastic decline. The paternalism that characterized all levels of Ming society— from the emperor's relations with his ministers to the landlords' rela-

This painting by an anonymous eighteenth-century artist gives an idealized view of the garden of a mansion in South China during the Ming Dynasty (1368–1644). Servants spin silk for weaving while a well-dressed young woman watches two children at play. In late imperial China, upper-class women were expected to live quiet, genteel lives within the confines of the family home.

tions with the peasantry—had degenerated into autocracy at the top and exploitation at the bottom of society. Merchants, limited largely to internal commerce and hemmed in by government regulations, had few opportunities to contribute to further national economic growth. Tax evasion and imperial extravagance began to strain the treasury. Over 100,000 imperial clansmen—every male descendant of Zhu Yuanzhang—were receiving government stipends by the end of the Ming period. The construction and furnishing of the tomb of the Wanli Emperor, who died in 1620, is estimated to have cost one half of an entire year's national income. Thus the familiar cycle of rising land taxes, lower revenues, and hard-pressed peasants began again. The administration, too, was showing severe signs of strain. Thousands of eunuchs serving in the imperial palace were used by the late Ming emperors as a kind of private civil service, bypassing the regular bureaucracy; they were feared and hated by the scholar-officials. The censorate began to become corrupt and inefficient; factionalism broke out within bureaucratic ranks.

When the Jesuit missionary Matteo Ricci arrived in Beijing from Macao in 1600—the first European seen in the Chinese capital in two and a half centuries—he and his followers found much to admire, despite dynastic decline. The glowing reports that the Jesuit fathers sent back home helped to spark an enduring wave of European enthusiasm for Chinese philosophy and decorative arts. After 1620 even the optimistic Jesuits became alarmed by news of rebellion in the countryside. Even more ominously, a new threat was beginning to arise on the northeastern frontier. The Manchus, under their great leader Nurhachi, had formed a tribal confederation and were beginning to expand their territorial control. By 1629 they were inside the Great Wall; in 1637 they took control of Korea. In 1644 an anti-Ming rebel army seized Beijing; the Chinese general in command unwisely asked the Manchus for help in crushing the rebellion. The Manchus retook the capital and declined to leave; the last Ming emperor hanged himself in his garden. The Manchu Qing Dynasty had begun, and over the next 20 years brought all of China into its domain.

A remnant of the Ming Dynasty lingered for a while, as a Ming prince fled to Taiwan in an attempt to regroup his forces and organize resist-

A new observatory, with European-style instruments, was built in Beijing in the 1660s by the Jesuit missionary Ferdinand Verbiest. During the early stages of contact between China and Europe, an exchange of ideas and techniques flowed in both directions on the basis of mutual respect.

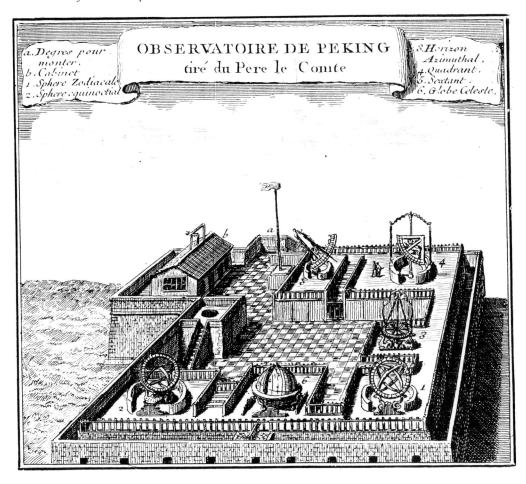

ance to the Manchus. He was aided by the patriotic pirate Zheng Chenggong, who drove the Dutch out of Taiwan in 1661 (they had built a fort there in the 1620s); soon, however, even this resistance was overcome by China's new rulers.

The Qing Dynasty

With the reign of the Kangxi Emperor in 1662, the Qing Dynasty began to implement a careful plan to ensure the success of their rule in China. Realizing, as the Mongols had done, that they were a tiny conquering minority and would have to maintain their ethnic cohesiveness, they organized Manchu tribesmen into hereditary military forces (called Banner Armies), forbade Manchu women to bind their daughters' feet, and ensured that all official documents were written in both Chinese and Manchu. Manchus continued to wear their own distinctive clothing, and were prohibited from marrying Chinese; all Chinese men had to wear their hair in a queue as a sign of submission.

At the same time, unlike the Mongols, the Manchus knew the value of governing China by Chinese methods, and set up their dynastic government as an almost exact replica of the Ming state. Any expression of anti-Manchu sentiment on the part of the scholar-officials brought immediate, harsh punishment. Many members of the Chinese elite expressed their loyalty to Chinese values indirectly, by retiring to lives of classical scholarship. But those who cooperated with the conquerors found that the Manchu rulers were, as a matter of policy, firm upholders of Neo-Confucian values and generous patrons of the arts.

From 1662 to 1796, the Qing Dynasty was ruled by three great emperors: Kangxi (1662–1723), Yongzheng (1723–1736), and Qianlong (1736–1796). True to the autocratic tendencies of the Ming, they maintained close control over their realm. European missionaries, increasingly seen as more subversive than useful, were put under severe restrictions. After 1742 most of them were expelled, except for a few who were employed by the court itself—such as Guiseppe Castiglione, court painter and architect to the Qianlong Emperor. A project in the 1730s to publish an imperial edition of the entire body of Chinese literature was a great boon to scholarship, but it was also a literary inquisition: any book judged not worthy of inclusion was burned by the censors. The censorate became not just a supervisory body, but also a secret service, alert to any hint of subversion.

If the three great Qing emperors were despots, their despotism was largely benevolent; their country was well ruled. By the early years of the Kangxi reign, China encompassed an area somewhat larger even than its present borders. The Manchus asserted their control over Tibet, Mongolia, and Xinjiang, and also (before losing them to Russia in the nineteenth century) the maritime provinces of Siberia east of the Ussuri River. The wealth of that vast territory was mobilized to create a larger and wealthier Chinese state than ever before. Tea, furs, and other luxury goods were traded overland to Russia; southern China grew wealthy with the growing export trade in tea, silk, and porcelain through Guangzhou to Europe. Early signs of industrialization (destined to be stifled during the dynasty's decline in the nineteenth century) were seen in all of China's large cities. The population, during that era of wealth and stability, grew rapidly once again, reaching 350 million by 1800.

The early Qing emperors appealed to the Manchu sentiments of their hereditary armies by going off to hunt on horseback in the northeast during the summer. They appealed to the Chinese elite by being perfect Confucian gentlemen. All three emperors were accomplished artists and enthusiastic art collectors, as the palace museums in Beijing and Taipei still attest today. Both the form and the ideology of Chinese government seemed to justify the pride that the ruling class took in them. Any citizen of China in the eighteenth century could quite honestly feel that he or she lived in the largest, richest, best-governed country in history.

At the same time, two forces were beginning quietly to undermine the foundations of late imperial China: overpopulation, and the encroachment of the west. Population growth, which for a long time had seemed like a source of new manpower and thus new wealth, was beginning to become a problem by the end of the eighteenth century. In some areas hunger was usual and famine was no longer uncommon. The administration, too, was burdened by population growth. Counties that might have been administered efficiently with a population of 20,000 could not cope with five or ten times that number. Carelessly, the government did not reorganize district lines to account for population growth. The bureaucracy itself was growing somewhat stagnant, compounding the problem of governing a huge population. The examination system rewarded plodding memorization more than intelligence; civil servants were less often well-motivated Confucian scholars, and more often slightly corrupt, overly cautious drones. Military weakness similarly compounded the problem of maintaining public order. When a rebellion led by the White Lotus secret society broke out in the 1790s, the hereditary "Banner Armies" showed that they had become lazy and incompetent, and took ten years to defeat the rebels.

Many of the problems that China faces in the late twentieth century —overpopulation, the need for political reform and for modernization in education, industry, and the military, and the search for an appropriate role in international affairs—already needed to be addressed at the end of the eighteenth century. Any hope of dealing with them at that time, however, was quickly overwhelmed by the need to cope with the increasingly aggressive demands of the west. Europeans had been trading in South China since the early sixteenth century, buying luxury goods in a commerce that was lucrative to local merchants but economically insignificant on a national scale. During the eighteenth century that situation changed, and a large-scale commodity trade began to develop, with serious consequences. The change was caused by an insatiable English thirst for tea.

In the 1730s, in an effort to control the growing trade with the west, the Qing Dynasty had set up a system of regulated trade in Guangzhou. Under the "Canton System," foreigners could live only in Macao and trade only at Guangzhou (Canton); they could deal only with certain licensed Chinese merchants who controlled all international trade. Throughout the century, British merchants came to dominate the trade between Europe and China, as they bought more and more tea to satisfy the demand at home. By the end of the century the tax on tea accounted for one-third of British crown revenue from foreign trade; but for the British economy as a whole, the drain of silver from England to China was a serious problem. The trade was almost all in one direction; the Chinese had little interest in European goods. (The main English export commodity was wool, which the Chinese regarded as a "barbarian" fabric.) The British would soon find a commodity—opium—to balance the trade, but they also attempted to find a diplomatic solution to their problem (which the Chinese government regarded as no problem at all).

Pressed by merchants who worried about the one-sidedness of the tea trade and who hated the restrictions and red tape of the Canton System, King George III in 1793 sent an embassy to Beijing to discuss the problem. His envoy, Lord MacCartney, presented a list of proposals, including the establishment of a free-trade system and western-style mutual diplomatic recognition, with an exchange of ambassadors in both directions. The Qianlong Emperor, who regarded Europeans as "barbarians" and their trade as "tribute," refused to consider the proposals. He sent MacCartney away with a letter to George III, urging the king to be "even more humble and submissive in the future."

The emperor's serene self-confidence was misplaced. Within a few years it would give way to a century of national humiliation at the hands of the west. By the early nineteenth century China's modern era of defeat, reaction, and revolution had begun. The Qing Dynasty would linger on until 1911, but even as the aging Qianlong Emperor sent his letter to George III, imperial China—proud, self-sufficient, and impervious to the rest of the world—was about to disappear forever.

The Structure of Traditional Chinese Society

When Confucius was asked, twenty-five centuries ago, how to bring perfect order to society, he replied, "Let fathers be fathers, let sons be sons." He assumed that the family was the basic unit of society. If every family was properly organized (with the duties and rights of both superiors and inferiors understood and respected), society as a whole would be properly organized too. The whole fabric of society was modeled on the proper relationship between fathers and sons.

Nowadays, in America, the word *family* refers to a small and simple structure: a married couple and their children. In traditional China, however, a family was a much larger and more complex social unit. Ideally, a house would consist of a walled compound enclosing several interconnected courtyards surrounded by inward-facing buildings. This

Traditional houses in Changsha, central China. All buildings face inward toward a central courtyard, emphasizing the solidarity of the family as the basic unit of Chinese society.

compound was home to an extended family consisting of a grandfather, his principal wife and one or more secondary wives, his sons and unmarried daughters, his sons' wives and children, servants, and various poor cousins, unmarried aunts, and so on. Such a household could easily consist of fifty or sixty people; it was ruled with absolute authority by the grandfather, advised by his adult sons.

Of course, such a large household was characteristic only of relatively rich people in traditional China. For most people the resident family unit was much smaller: grandparents, the eldest married son, and his wife and children. Other married sons would live separately; they still were expected, however, to accept their father's advice in most matters.

Whether it was large or small, every traditional family could be described by three technical terms used by anthropologists: *patriarchal*, *patrilineal*, and *patrilocal*.

Patriarchal means that the family was ruled by the oldest living male. Within the household high-status women—particularly widowed grandmothers—often had considerable power and authority, but in the end the patriarch's word was law. A grandfather or father expected his orders to be obeyed; any disobedience was considered shockingly immoral. Filial piety, the duty and respect owed by a son to his ancestors, was the most important moral principle in Chinese society. The patriarch was expected to make his decisions on the basis of the best interests of the family as a whole. The individual wishes of members of the family were of much lesser importance. The head of the family told his children when and whom to marry, whether to go to school or go to work, and whether (and on what) they could spend money. By focusing social responsibility on the family, the Chinese system limited individual initiative, but also relieved individuals of the anxiety of making important decisions on their own and fostered a sense of group solidarity.

In a *patrilineal* system, descent is traced only through the male side of the family. A man was known not just as an individual, but as the descendant of his male ancestors. All but the poorest families had small family shrines inside their houses, in which the names of ancestors for several generations were written on small wooden tablets. The head of the family would place offerings on the shrine on religious holidays, and would make a formal announcement of important family events—such as births, weddings, and deaths—in front of the shrine. The head of the family was also responsible for making sure that the family graves were maintained in good condition. These duties had to be performed by a man; thus, a family that failed to produce a son would eventually cease to exist.

An elderly couple in Shanghai. Old people enjoy great respect and authority in Chinese society.

In China's *patrilocal* family system, when a woman married, she ceased to be a member of her parents' family; married women always lived with their husband's parents. A bride was expected to accept her mother-in-law as her own new mother and to obey her absolutely. If any dispute arose, a husband would always side with his mother rather than with his wife. A young married woman would have low status and little security within her new family until she gave birth to a son. At that point, she would be honored for helping to continue the family line.

A woman's shift from her family of birth to her family of marriage was absolute. Marriage was prohibited between two people with the same surname, so a bride was unlikely to have any close relatives in her new family; often, marriage would take her to live in a new village. She would rarely visit her parents after her marriage. Only if she were divorced would she return to live with her parents, and that was uncommon and a source of great disgrace. If her husband died, she would remain with his family. Widows rarely remarried; it was considered far more honorable for a widow to remain faithful to her husband's memory.

Sons were much more highly valued than daughters in traditional Chinese families, because a daughter's long-term contribution to her family was limited. Naturally, daughters were loved, appreciated, and well cared for as individuals, but as the Chinese said, "Raising daughters is like raising children for another family." In times of extreme stress, such as a prolonged famine, daughters might be sold as servants or prostitutes, or even killed, in order to give sons a better chance for survival. Such drastic steps would cause the parents great emotional suffering; still, the survival of the family line was more important than any individual in the family.

Girls rarely received much formal education. Their training was limited to cooking, household management, and such skills as weaving and embroidery. Good training was an asset in arranging a girl's marriage. Marriages were arranged by the parents of the prospective bride and groom, usually with the help and advice of a go-between. The two people most directly involved were not consulted, and in fact might meet for the first time at their wedding. The bride was expected to bring to her new family a dowry of household goods and, perhaps, land—another reason daughters were regarded as a useless expense.

In general, the status of women declined over the long run in Chinese history. Prior to the Song Dynasty (960–1279) it was not uncommon for women, at least in wealthy families, to be well educated and have a certain amount of independent social life. Their relative loss of inde-

Woman's shoe, late nineteenth century, reproduced actual size. The rather plain decoration indicates that its owner was not a member of the upper class. Her bound foot was about four inches long, larger than was considered ideal.

pendence thereafter was the result of a decline in aristocratic values and the rise of the more conservative gentry-bureaucratic class. Certainly the inferior and dependent status of women was symbolized by the peculiar custom of foot-binding.

Although the precise origins of the custom are unclear, foot-binding began sometime in the eleventh century. It was found first among the upper classes, but eventually spread to the majority of the population. When a girl reached the age of around five years old, her mother would wrap her feet tightly in long bands of cloth, bending the toes under the sole of the foot and forcing the arch into a high curve. The tight wrappings, maintained throughout childhood and adolescence, prevented the feet from achieving their normal growth. The resulting tiny, misshapen feet were regarded as physically beautiful. Bound feet were essential if a girl were to achieve a good marriage. A woman with bound feet was partly crippled, and so bound feet were a badge of wealth and status: They proclaimed that a family could afford to keep women who were incapable of hard physical labor. Bound feet prevented women from going very far from home, because it was impossible for them to walk unaided for more than a short distance. Foot-binding, a symbol of women's pain and oppression for centuries, was finally outlawed at the end of the Qing Dynasty.

Class Structure

Around 300 B.C. the Confucian philosopher Mencius observed that:

some people labor with their minds, and some with their strength. Those who labor with their minds govern others; those who labor with their strength are governed by others. . . . This is a principle universally recognized.

Traditional Chinese society did not believe that all people were equal. Differences in class status, wealth, and quality of life were considered natural. At the same time, all classes were considered to make some contribution to society. The ruling class ranked first; they believed (and most other people went along with this) that their wealth and status was a natural reward for their superior talent and moral qualities, and for their assuming the burdens of government. Farmers, producers of food (and payers of grain tax), ranked next. Artisans, who produced nonfood goods, ranked third; fourth and last came merchants, who produced nothing but only moved goods around. Off the scale at the bottom of the social ladder were rootless laborers, actors, prostitutes, and others in the entertainment business, and workers in "unclean" occupations (such as butchers and tanners).

This theoretical description of class structure was only partly a reflection of reality. Traditional Chinese social theorists often complained, for example, that people of nominally low status often enjoyed great wealth and power; a rich merchant was in every way better off than a poor farmer. Still, theory corresponded to reality in three important ways. First, there was no doubt about the superior position of the ruling class, the landowning, literate, degree-holding members of the bureaucracy. Second, the owning of agricultural land was the foundation of wealth and prestige; rich merchants, for example, would often invest in land rather than put profits back into their own businesses. This tended to reinforce the traditional structure of power, and to retard the growth of an independent, entrepreneurial merchant class. (In Renaissance and early modern Europe, landowning also had great prestige, but both nations and individuals grew wealthy through trade.) Third, a person's class was a reflection of his work; social mobility in both directions was possible. The son of any "respectable" family could take the civil service examinations, and success would immediately raise him and his family to the top of the social ladder.

Of course, it was not easy for a young man from a poor family to get the education necessary to pass the examinations. But it was not impossible, and the support structure of the extended family created some

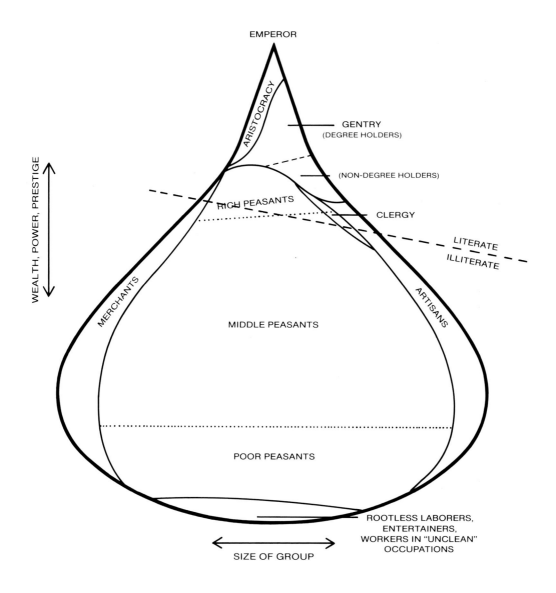

Diagram of the structure of society in late traditional China. Wealth, power, and prestige are indicated on the vertical scale; numbers of people in each group are indicated by width on the horizontal scale.

opportunities. A very talented poor boy, for example, might be supported and educated by a rich uncle. This was an investment in the future; if the boy passed the examinations, the entire family would benefit. This type of direct social mobility was possible only for men, however. Women took the social class first of their fathers, and then of their husbands.

There were important differences in status within social classes. Within the ruling class, for example, there was the hereditary aristocracy (which declined in size and influence over time, but did not entirely disappear), followed by powerful national officials, and then by other members of the bureaucracy. Below them were holders of the lowest examination degree, many of whom would never hold office. At the bottom of the ruling class were rich landlords who did not have civil service rank but who possessed considerable influence on a local level. Within the agricultural class were small landlords and rich peasants—families with a surplus of land, who derived some of their income from renting land to others; then middle peasants, who owned an adequate amount of land (and perhaps rented additional fields from others); then poor peasants, who rented most or all of their land from others. Merchants ranged from wealthy dealers in grain and cloth to peddlers who traveled from one town fair to another. The artisan class included wealthy individuals who produced such goods as porcelain or furniture on a large scale as well as village-level potters and blacksmiths. Chinese society was complex and dynamic, with networks of wealth, status and power at the local, regional, and national levels.

The Structure of Government

Chinese theories of government saw the empire as a great family, with the emperor as its patriarch. Just as the head of a family served as its

Mao Zedong was born in this comfortable farmhouse in Shaoshan, Hunan Province. As rich peasants, his parents enjoyed considerable standing in the local community, and could afford to give their son a good education.

intermediary with the ancestors, the emperor was the Son of Heaven; he embodied the point of contact between heaven and earth, the natural and the human worlds. As the holder of the Mandate of Heaven, the emperor was responsible for maintaining harmony and order throughout the universe. He did so by presiding over a government that was paternalistic and benevolent, ensuring every subject his or her rightful place in the social order.

Although the structure of imperial government changed in many details over the course of time, its general outlines persisted from the Han period to the fall of the last dynasty in 1911. The emperor was the head of the government. All male descendants of the founder of a dynasty had aristocratic titles, but not necessarily any real power. The

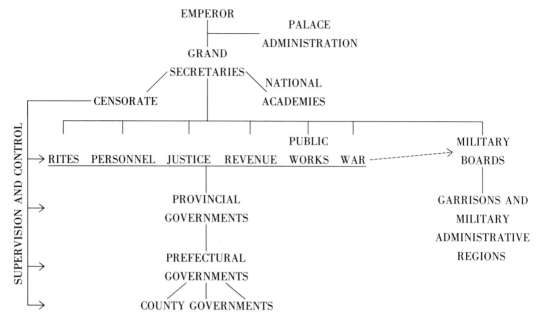

Organization of Chinese government under the Ming Dynasty.

day-to-day supervision of the government was handled by a prime minister (or, in the Ming and Qing periods, one or more grand secretaries). The imperial palace—an establishment housing not only the emperor and his wives, but also thousands of concubines, eunuchs, and servants—had its own separate administration. The national government itself consisted of six ministries: rites (handling religious and ceremonial affairs), personnel, justice, revenue, public works, and war. The ministry of war was a civilian agency; the actual military command structure was headed by several military boards, which reported to the grand secretaries. Below the national government were about twenty provinces, each headed by a governor; military garrisons and certain strategic border regions were controlled by military governors. Each province was divided into several prefectures, and each prefecture into several counties. The national government also included several academies, "think tanks" that carried out special research projects and drafted important documents for the emperor. Another arm of the central government, of particular interest and importance, was the censorate: an independent agency that operated at all levels of government to audit accounts, pay surprise inspection visits to other government offices, and conduct undercover operations to detect corruption and inefficiency. Senior censors were also expected—sometimes at great risk to themselves—to criticize the emperor when they disapproved of his actions.

The county magistrate, occupying the lowest rung on the ladder of the imperial bureaucracy, was the key to uniform national administration. As degree holders, magistrates shared the same training and outlook; they applied the same set of laws and regulations nationwide. Magistrates were rotated frequently from one post to another, and (in order to avoid corruption) were prohibited from serving in their home prefectures. The magistrate was responsible for a wide range of duties: the assessment and collection of taxes, the detection of crime and administration of justice, the mobilization of the local militia, the upkeep of public works, and the performance of ritual and ceremonial functions. He was also expected to organize the local ruling class in support of the government.

In the magistrate's office (called a *yamen*), large registers were kept showing the ownership of all of the land in the county. These were used as the basis for collecting taxes, which were paid in grain in ancient times but in silver from the Ming Dynasty onward. The magistrate would keep a portion of the tax revenue to cover local expenses and forward the remainder to the prefecture. There, a portion again would be kept for expenses, and the rest sent on to the provincial government, and so on.

The yamen also had a courtroom, where citizens could present petitions and make complaints, and where civil and criminal cases were tried. It was expensive and difficult to present a civil case; the government much preferred that people should settle their disputes privately. The magistrate was, however, required to investigate all crimes reported in his county and to arrest criminals for trial. No conviction was possible without a confession, and suspects could be tortured to force them to confess. (This had also been the case under Roman law.) Witnesses were likely to be questioned very harshly. On the other hand, a magistrate who convicted someone falsely was subject to severe punishment, as was anyone who made a false accusation about someone else. Punishment for crimes could range from flogging, forced labor, and exile to execution. Difficult cases—and all cases involving capital punishment—were referred to higher levels of government for review. In general, justice in traditional China was stern, but not unfair.

Clearly, a magistrate's job was more than any single individual could handle. A magistrate usually had several personal assistants, paid out of his own funds, who accompanied him from one post to the next. Each yamen also had its local staff of clerks, policemen, messengers, and so on; they were not imperial employees, but were paid out of local tax revenues. Magistrates came and went, but yamen employees stayed on; and despite their low status, they often had great power locally. They also were often arbitrary and corrupt and were much resented by the local people. Neighborhoods, villages, guilds, and other organizations had headmen appointed by the magistrate to assist in maintaining order.

The magistrate also had to enlist the help of the local gentry in performing his duties. Members of the gentry were expected to contribute time and money to such things as maintaining roads, canals, and other public works; soup kitchens and other public charities; and the organization of a local militia. They also assisted the magistrate in his

A Society Without Lawyers

The imperial government of China deeply disapproved of lawyers, whom it regarded as "tricksters" who encouraged people to file lawsuits rather than settling cases informally within their own communities. When cases did come to court, people were expected to plead their own causes, without the advice of lawyers. Anyone who encouraged another person to file a lawsuit was subject to punishment. The following ruling was handed down by the Qing Dynasty's Ministry of Justice in 1820, confirming a ruling of the lower courts:

The governor of Anhui Province has reported a case in which Xu Xuechuan, an offender from another province, drafted five litigation documents for other persons. All of these documents were of an ordinary nature, and there is no evidence that he conspired with government clerks, tricked ignorant country folk, or practiced intimidation or fraud.

He should therefore receive a one-degree lesser penalty, namely three years' penal servitude, rather than the military exile which is prescribed for habitual litigation tricksters.

Although the offender is past the age of seventy, since he is a litigation specialist who brings harm to rural communities, he may not be allowed the privilege of monetary redemption for his offense.

Adapted from: Derk Bodde and Clarence Morris, *Law in Imperial China* (Cambridge: Harvard University Press, 1973), pp. 415–416. Reprinted with permission.

ritual duties, such as the annual ceremonies that were held at the temple of Confucius. As much as possible, the government relied on local and informal social institutions to carry out many public functions. Village headmen, for example, were supposed to intervene in private disputes between people in their villages, so as to prevent legal cases from being brought to court.

Certain functions of government did not come under the authority of magistrates. Large public works, for example, like the Grand Canal or major port facilities, were supervised directly by departments of the Ministry of Public Works. Similarly, the supervisors of the imperial porcelain factories and the Salt Administration reported directly to the national government. The military also operated outside the network of civilian government, although it was under the overall control of the Ministry of War. There was a separate military bureaucracy, with professional officers and conscripted or volunteer troops. Officers, who were entitled to wear splendid ceremonial armor, were recruited through a separate examination system; but military careers were usually regarded as less desirable than civilian careers. Under the Qing Dynasty, this system changed. Most military men, both officers and soldiers, held hereditary rank in the Banner Armies; most of them were descendants of the Manchu conquerors who founded the dynasty. Local militias supplemented the regular army, but were usually used only for minor functions such as the suppression of bandits.

The imperial government generally seemed quite remote to most ordinary Chinese. Social control rested primarily with local institutions, and with a widely shared conception of what society should be like and what was expected of people. Any behavior that was disruptive, or even just individualistic, was quickly brought back into line, beginning within the family itself. As the Confucian classic *The Great Learning* said:

*The ancient kings who wished to shine forth their illustrious virtue through-
out the kingdom first ordered well their own states. Wishing to order well
their states, they first regulated their families.*

In traditional China, the family was a small version of the state, the state
a large version of the family. When each was in good order, the result
was a stable, conservative, and harmonious society.

Religion
and Philosophy

The great era of Chinese philosophy was nearly contemporary with that of Greece: from about 500 to 100 B.C. During that span of four centuries, a number of famous thinkers established the main lines of thought that would guide Chinese intellectual history for another two thousand years. Those thinkers themselves, however, drew on a common heritage that stretched back to the dawn of Chinese civilization itself.

There were a number of ideas on which virtually everyone in China could agree. The universe was uncreated, and time extended infinitely into both the past and the future. The universe was organic—everything was connected to everything else—and existed in a basic state of harmony. Heaven (not simply the sky, nor a sky god, but the sum of all natural forces) both affected and was affected by human conduct. The family was the basic unit of human society, and duties to the ancestors took priority over everything else. Civilization was the invention of human genius, embodied in a few sage-kings of ancient times; the goal of government was to adhere to the values of civilization as the ancients had defined them. Heaven's mandate to a ruler allowed him and his descendants to rule as long as they maintained cosmic harmony and good government. Gods and ancestors could give guidance to humans (and especially to rulers) if they were worshiped and consulted with appropriate rituals.

Up until the middle of the Zhou Dynasty (1059–221 B.C.), this ancient wisdom was never clearly formulated. Rather, it represented the common system of beliefs of a relatively stable aristocratic, feudal society. That belief system was expressed in a variety of myths and legends, historical chronicles, poems and songs, religious rituals, books of fortune-telling, and an unwritten code of personal conduct familiar to every member of the ruling class. By the middle of the Zhou period, however, the old order was breaking down, and so the beliefs that had supported it were called into question. The authority of the Zhou kings was increasingly ignored; rulers of the feudal states acted as independent kings. Large states conquered and swallowed up small ones; rulers were driven from their thrones by their own ministers and generals. This situation of dangerous political instability prompted a number of thinkers to enquire more closely into the nature of human society and universal order, so as to find a way to bring harmony to the world once again.

Confucius and His Followers

Confucius (551–479 B.C.), like many early Chinese philosophers, was a member of the lower ranks of the aristocracy, a class whose existence

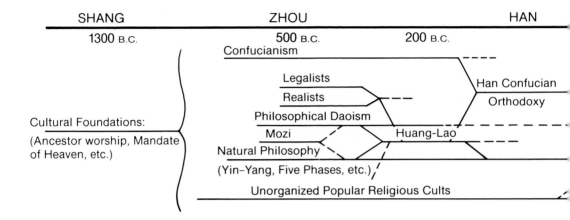

SOLID HORIZONTAL LINES = DOMINANT SCHOOL(S) AT ANY GIVEN TIME

BROKEN HORIZONTAL LINES = SECONDARY SCHOOL(S) AT ANY GIVEN TIME

SOLID SLANTED LINES = STRONG INFLUENCE

BROKEN SLANTED LINES = LESSER INFLUENCE

Historical Development of Chinese Religion and Philosophy

was made dangerous and uncertain by the political changes of the time. After a brief and not very successful career as an advisor to the ruler of his native state of Lu (in present Shandong Province), he gave up government service to become a teacher. Because he never achieved a position of influence as a high government official, he regarded himself as a failure; but later ages have considered him the greatest philosopher in Chinese history.

As a teacher, Confucius tried to train a large number of followers to be advisors to the rulers of their day, so as to change the way the world was run. He did not see himself as a reformer, but rather as a conservative who was trying to restore the ethical, benevolent government of

DISUNION		TANG	SONG	YUAN	MING	QING	PRESENT
A.D. 200		A.D. 700	A.D. 1100	A.D. 1300	A.D. 1500	A.D. 1800	20TH CENTURY

Religious Daoism

trology, alchemy, medicine)

Buddhism

Various Buddhist Sects

Popular Religions

Nestorian Christianity

Catholicism & Protestantism

Islam

Modern Western Ideologies

ancient times. In fact, however, he created a genuinely new way of thinking about society and government in China, even though he described it in terms of an idealized past.

The understanding that true nobility was a product of virtue, rather than of aristocratic birth, was Confucius's greatest contribution to Chinese social philosophy. His ideal was the *junzi*, a word that literally means "son of a prince," but which for Confucius signified a "perfect gentleman." His "son of a prince" was anyone who behaved in a princely way, regardless of his birth. For Confucius, the perfect gentleman was characterized by the "five virtues": *ren*, "benevolence" or "empathy"; *yi*, "righteousness"; *li*, "proper conduct"; *zhi*, "understanding"; and *xin*, "trustworthiness." Together these five added up to the supreme virtue of *xiao*, "filial piety," the duties owed to one's parents and ancestors. Confucius held that anyone could cultivate these virtues through study and self-discipline; he insisted that only the virtuous deserved to be rulers. Confucius taught that if the world is to be harmonious, words and reality must correspond; a king is truly a king only if he acts like a king.

Written codes of law were being introduced in some of the feudal states of China during Confucius's lifetime. Confucius was very much opposed to them. He felt that laws would simply define some people as criminals, without doing anything to reform them, and also that written laws would inspire clever people to find loopholes in the law. He felt instead that self-cultivation would lead naturally to proper conduct, both in personal and in public life. Proper conduct on the part of rulers would be imitated by ordinary people, producing a society that had no need for laws.

Confucius's two best-known followers were Mengzi (Mencius; 372–289 B.C.) and Xunzi (3rd century B.C.). Mengzi was an idealist. He taught that human nature is good, and that goodness should be the basis of government. Good government would succeed, he taught, because people respond naturally to goodness; they would support a virtuous ruler but abandon a wicked one. Xunzi was less optimistic. He believed that human nature was at best neutral, but that people could be made good through education. Some people, however, would reject the opportunity to be good, and would have to be controlled through laws and punishments. Both the idealistic and the pragmatic versions of Confucius's teachings played a role in the later development of Confucianism.

Many westerners have wondered whether Confucianism is a religion or a philosophy. The Chinese sidestep the issue by referring to it simply as a "teaching." Confucius certainly believed in some kind of an after-

Confucius and Mencius

The name Confucius is a Latinized form of Kongfuzi, "Great Master Kong." The teachings of Confucius were collected and written down by his disciples after his death, in the form of brief lessons and conversations:

The Master said, "The mind of the superior man is occupied with righteousness; the mind of the inferior man is occupied with gain."

The later followers of Confucius often wrote essays and commentaries expanding on the brief lessons that survive in the Master's own words. The opening chapter of the book of Mencius (Mengzi) is a famous example:

Mencius went to see King Hui of Liang. The king said, "Sir, you have not minded coming a thousand leagues to see me. I assume you have some message that will be profitable for my kingdom."

Mencius replied, "Why do you use the word profit? I have come to teach about benevolence and righteousness, and those are my only topics.

"If you say, 'What can be done to profit my kingdom?' your great officers will say, 'What can be done to profit our families?' and your lesser officers and the common people will say, 'What can be done to profit ourselves?' Superiors and inferiors will all try to snatch profit from each other, and the kingdom will be endangered. . . .

Your majesty likewise should say, 'Benevolence and righteousness, these are my only topics.' Why must you use the word profit?"

life; that was the basis of the ancient cult of ancestors, which Confucius firmly upheld. But his goal was not religious salvation, but rather the full realization *in this life* of the human potential for wisdom and virtue. Confucianism is, fundamentally, a way of life: one that has had a profound impact on China and all of East Asia, right up to the present day.

The Rivals of Confucianism

Confucius and his immediate followers had many rivals in trying to find solutions to the problems of civil war and social breakdown that dominated the Warring States Period. Mozi, an elder contemporary of Mengzi, rejected family loyalty and preached universal love; he taught that wars should be fought only in self-defense. (Understandably, given the conditions of the time, no rulers took his advice.) Some philosophers looked to logic to provide the basis for a stable political order. Others investigated the natural world—astronomy, mathematics, topography, and so on—to try to understand man's place in the cosmic order. Most of these philosophers failed to create long-lasting ideologies, but they nevertheless were important contributors to the intellectual life of their time. The Warring States Period was an age of vigorous debate and unusual openness to new ideas.

A group of thinkers known as Legalists had a significant impact on political theory at that time. Shang Yang and his follower, Han Feizi, contended that virtue had nothing to do with government. People, they said, were motivated only by fear and greed, and so government should be founded on punishments and rewards. If laws were clear and precise, punishments terrifying, and rewards prompt, people would do exactly what the government wanted them to. Government would be virtually automatic, leaving the emperor free to enjoy himself in his palace. As the First Emperor of Qin found, however, Legalism did not work in practice.

Another group of Legalists, now usually called the Realists, were less interested in law itself than in administrative policy. They taught that a ruler would be secure if he were fair, moderate, militarily strong, and good at choosing his officials. They also relied on astrology to select favorable times for the ruler to take action. The Realists were very much in favor of the practice—first adopted by the southern state of Chu in the fourth century B.C., and later a standard part of imperial bureaucratic rule—of appointing officials to govern provinces and counties, rather than relying on hereditary aristocrats.

Nothing at all is known about Laozi, but his book, the *Dao De Jing* ("The Way and Its Power"), is the most important work in the school of philosophy called Daoism. (It is also well known in the West, and has been translated into English many times.) His ideal ruler was a superhuman sage, so completely attuned to the Dao (cosmic unity, or, as we might say, the Force) that he governed without effort. His people, kept well-fed and ignorant, would live happily in their villages, unaware that they were even being governed. Another great early Daoist, Juangzi, lived around 300 B.C. He was nearly an anarchist; he felt that there was no valid way of making judgments in a world where everything is relative. The only safe course, he said, was for a person to cultivate oneness with nature and avoid wordly entanglements. Juangzi's message was completely impractical as a recipe for social order, but it did provide some comfort for generations of failed or retired Chinese bureaucrats, who liked to think of themselves as "hermits" writing poetry and contemplating nature in their "thatched huts." Daoism's lyrical, subjective attitude toward nature had a powerful influence on the development of Chinese art.

Juangzi

Juangzi ridiculed the efforts of his fellow philosophers to create a government that would work. Humans, he said, are only a tiny part of a vast universe; any effort to create a human-centered world is bound to fail. His answer was *wuwei*, "taking no action contrary to nature." Like a Zhou Dynasty hippie, he wanted to "go with the flow." He was fond of putting his lessons into the form of stories:

Once Juangzi dreamed that he was a butterfly—a butterfly flitting around, doing as it wishes, enjoying itself. Suddenly he woke up. He couldn't tell if he had been Juangzi dreaming that he was a butterfly, or if he was a butterfly dreaming that he was Juangzi. But mustn't there be some difference between Juangzi and a butterfly? This is called the transformability of things.

Juangzi was walking in the mountains when he saw a huge tree. A woodcutter passed by, but made no move to cut down the tree. Juangzi asked why, and he said, "The wood of this kind of tree is not useful for anything. It's a worthless tree." Juangzi said, "Because of its worthlessness, this tree is able to stay alive for a long time."

Juangzi said, "As I was walking along, I heard someone calling to me. There was a fish lying in a rut in the road. The fish said, 'Will you give me a dipperful of water?' I replied, 'How about if I divert the course of the West River so that it will flow in this direction?' The fish replied, 'If you give me a dipperful of water, I can stay alive. But if we follow your plan, you may as well look for me in a dried-fish shop.' "

Juangzi made no contributions to the Chinese art of government, but his stories have retained their vitality because of their emphasis on the value of keeping things in perspective.

The Han Dynasty Synthesis

In the lively intellectual world of the late Warring States Period, philosophers constantly experimented with taking ideas from earlier thinkers and combining them to create new systems of thought. Flexibility was much more important than doctrinal rigidity. Nevertheless, broadly speaking, the philosophies of that time may be organized into three general categories: Confucianism, Legalism/Realism, and Daoism. Confucianism was often regarded as too idealistic to be practical, but was admired for its attention to the lessons of history and its ethical consciousness. Despotic Legalism was completely discredited by the First Emperor of Qin's experiment in a rigid government of laws, but Realism offered useful advice on how to run a government. Daoism appealed to rulers because of its emphasis on the king as a superhuman sage tuned in to the rhythms of the universe.

By the early Han Dynasty (second century B.C.), Realism and Daoism merged to form the Huang-Lao school of philosophy. The name is derived from Huang Di, the legendary Yellow Emperor of antiquity, and Laozi. Huang Di was associated with the Mandate of Heaven, astrology, alchemy, and the notion that the ruler was the unique meeting point between heaven and earth, the natural and the human realms. Laozi symbolized the sage-king's use of spiritual powers to get other people to do his bidding. Huang-Lao philosophy dominated Chinese intellectual life during the first decades of the Han Dynasty.

Around 100 B.C., Dong Zhongshu, court philosopher to Emperor Wu of the Han, merged Huang-Lao philosophy with Confucianism, creating a new form of Confucianism that was family centered, ethical, and based on tradition, but which also paid attention to administrative realities and a sense that Chinese dynastic rule was part of a vast cosmic plan. This revised Confucianism became established as a state-sponsored or-

The Forbidden City in Beijing is a vast complex of palaces, gardens, and ceremonial pavilions, designed to embody the grandeur and authority of China's emperors. The audience hall in this photo is surrounded by auspicious symbols, such as the crane, emblem of long life and spiritual wisdom.

thodoxy; for a thousand years it formed the basis for the training and selection of government officials. Dong Zhongshu thus occupies a position in Chinese philosophy comparable to that of Aristotle in the West: He created a comprehensive system of philosophy against which all other doctrines would have to be judged. A father-and-son team of editors, Liu Xiang and Liu Xin, also aided the establishment of orthodoxy by preparing standard editions of the classics.

During the three centuries of disunion that followed the fall of the

Han in A.D. 220, orthodox Han Confucianism to some extent lost its dominant position in Chinese intellectual life, as new doctrines arose to compete with it. Even so, it kept alive the ideal of the unified imperial state with a merit-based bureaucracy, and in the long run survived all challenges to its status as the basic doctrine of China's ruling class.

Religion in Ancient China

Ancestor worship, the fundamental religion of China, is based on the belief that the souls of the dead live on as spirits that can advise and influence the lives of their descendants. Every person was believed to have two souls: an earthly soul that was buried with the dead, and which required offerings to keep it satisfied in the grave, and a spiritual soul that departed from the body at death and needed to be worshiped and given periodic offerings to keep it happy and benevolent. A neglected soul might become a "hungry ghost," bringing misfortune to its careless descendants.

When a person died, rituals were conducted to try to call his or her soul back to its body. Only when those attempts failed could a funeral proceed. Large, expensive funerals were a sign of respect for the dead, as were large numbers of grave offerings. Vessels of bronze or clay were buried with the dead, along with servants for the afterlife. By the middle of the Zhou period, living sacrificial victims were usually replaced by wooden or clay substitutes (like the famous underground clay army of the First Emperor of Qin), but the amount and value of grave goods for a member of the ruling class could still be staggering.

Besides the ancestors, a variety of gods were worshiped in ancient China. Feudal rulers had temples to their ancestors, but also to the god of heaven, the god of the soil, and to local gods of rivers and mountains. Shamans—spiritual intermediaries—were employed to communicate with gods and dead ancestors. Among the common people, many different gods were worshiped, including some associated with fertility and good harvests. Religious rituals included music, dancing, and animal sacrifice.

The Search for Immortality

By the late Warring States Period, the idea that souls live on after death gave rise to the belief that it might be possible to postpone death indefinitely, and keep the earthly and spiritual souls united with the body forever. Means of accomplishing that included exercises and breathing techniques designed to nourish vital energy within the body, and also elixirs of immortality and various forms of magic. When death did occur, efforts were made to preserve bodies for as long as possible within the grave. Some noblemen were buried in suits made of jade scales (jade was believed to prevent decay); others were buried in airtight coffins in carefully sealed tombs. Jade suits did not work, but sealed tombs sometimes did. In 1973, for example, archaeologists excavated the tomb of the Lady of Dai, near Changsha. After she was buried, in 168 B.C., both decay and dehydration halted in about two weeks; her body was found in almost perfect condition two thousand years later.

The quest for immortality became a central element in Chinese religion from the late Warring States Period onward. It was elevated to an imperial cult during the Han, when an official temple was dedicated to the Queen Mother of the West, keeper of the elixir of immortality. Chinese alchemists began a centuries-long quest for chemicals that would contain "compressed time," enabling those who ingested them to live for centuries. (Many of those formulas were based on mercury or arsenic; they were highly poisonous, but also highly effective embalming agents. Anyone who ate them would die, but his or her corpse would not decay—attaining "immortality" of a sort.) From the Song Dynasty (960–1279) onward, chemical alchemy was largely replaced by "internal alchemy," the use of yoga and meditation to enhance longevity.

Religious Daoism

The Latter Han Dynasty (A.D. 25–220) was a time of great religious developments in China. Buddhism was introduced by missionaries from Central Asia around 50 A.D., and as it slowly developed a following in China, a second new religious movement began to take shape. Daoism was transformed from an elite philosophy to a full-scale religion.

Religious Daoism was founded during the second half of the second century A.D. by Zhang Daoling, who experienced a series of religious visions and began preaching the new doctrine that they revealed. Laozi was elevated to the status of a god, a sage who had achieved immortality. Zhang Daoling taught that others could follow his example through meditation, discipline, and religious faith. Zhang and his followers created an organized church with an ordained clergy (always headed by a direct descendant of the founder), rituals and liturgies, and a body of divinely inspired scripture. The various popular religions of the time were examined by the Daoist clergy; some were accepted into Daoism, while others (especially those that involved the sacrifice of living creatures) were rejected.

Daoism developed, over a period of centuries, a large body of written doctrine, a sophisticated theology, and a large pantheon of gods organized as a celestial bureaucracy that paralleled that of the Chinese government itself. Daoism was often closely associated with the alchemical search for immortality; it also emphasized an attitude of detachment from the vulgar world of affairs. From the end of the Han Dynasty into the Song Dynasty, it exerted a powerful hold on China's elite, but declined thereafter with the revival of Confucianism. Daoism was a popular religion as well as an elite one; it sometimes was associated with popular rebellions aimed at sweeping away the existing world order and replacing it with a religiously inspired society. For that reason, Daoism was often viewed with suspicion by orthodox Confucians.

Buddhism in China

The history of Buddhism in China can be divided into four periods: preparation, acceptance, success, and decline. The period of preparation lasted from Buddhism's introduction to China in the first century A.D. until the middle of the fourth century. During that long period, scriptures had to be translated from Sanskrit into Chinese, a whole new vocabulary of religious terminology invented (attempts to apply Daoist terms to Buddhist concepts led only to confusion), and the differences between Theravada and Mahayana doctrines (see box page 140) sorted out. Buddhist teachings struck many Chinese as strange, and—because Buddhism was preached by foreign missionaries—there was widespread suspicion of the new "barbarian" religion. On the other hand, the disordered time that followed the fall of Han persuaded many people of the truth of Buddhism's central message, that salvation could be found only through transcending the world and its suffering.

The period of acceptance may be dated from the late fourth century, when the Indian monk Kumarajiva translated more than ninety Bud-

A Daoist god rides on the head of a winged dragon. This figure, carved in stone on the walls of a cave temple near Kunming, dates from the Yuan Dynasty (1279–1368).

dhist scriptures into Chinese, and the Chinese monk Faxian made a pilgrimage to India to study at the fountainhead of the faith. The non-Chinese Toba rulers of the Wei Dynasty (386–534) in northern China became great patrons of Buddhism, using public funds to establish temples and monasteries. Temples and their landholdings, as well as individual monks, were granted exemption from taxation. During this period, the cave temples at Longmen (near Luoyang), Yungang (near Datong), and Dunhuang (on the Silk Route in western Gansu), with their magnificent stone sculptures and murals, became famous centers of Buddhist worship.

By the middle of the sixth century, Buddhism occupied a central place in the religious and intellectual life of China. For three hundred years Buddhism prospered, and in the process became thoroughly Chinese. New sects such as the Pure Land promised easy salvation, and gained millions of converts. Chan (Zen) Buddhism, with its emphasis on meditation and the arts, appealed to the literate upper classes. Buddhism spread from China to Korea and Japan, and had a profound long-term influence on those cultures; pilgrims from all over East Asia visited the great monastery at Mt. Tiantai, in Zhejiang Province.

During the Tang Dynasty, at the height of Buddhist success in China, Buddhism, Daoism, and Confucianism were to some extent rivals for the attention and religious faith of both the ruling class and the common people. But the Chinese attitude toward religion has usually been a broad-minded one, and most people saw no conflicts among the Three Teachings. A person might, for example, pray at the temple of Confucius before taking the civil service examinations, call in a Daoist doctor to cure an illness, and invite Buddhist priests to chant at a funeral.

An old monk studying the Buddhist scriptures, near Beijing, ca. 1920. Only his eyeglasses and magnifying glass give us a clue that this scene is set in modern times.

Buddhism

Buddhism originated as a reformed version of Brahmanism, the ancient religion of India. It was founded by Siddartha Gautama, who lived around 600 B.C. in what is now Nepal. A nobleman saddened by the suffering that he saw in the world around him, Gautama spent a long time in meditation, which enabled him to become a Buddha—a fully enlightened being. He taught his followers that the world has no reality; it is an illusion that only seems real because people want it to be so. Attachment to the illusion of reality inevitably produces suffering, and leads to an endless cycle of rebirths governed by *karma* (the accumulated weight of past existences). The only escape from the cycle of birth, old age, sickness, and death is Buddhahood, enlightenment in the *dharma* (truth). When a Buddha leaves this earthly life, he enters *nirvana*; his individual soul is merged into cosmic unity, the only true reality.

As an organized religion, Buddhism stresses devotion to the Three Treasures—Buddha, *dharma*, and *sangha* (the religious community). Its doctrine is summarized in the Four Noble Truths: All life is suffering; suffering comes from attachment to the world; attachment can be overcome; the means for overcoming attachment are discipline, good moral conduct, and meditation. The teachings of Buddhism are contained in *sutras*, scriptures that all supposedly represent the words of Gautama Buddha, although many of them were written long after his death. Buddhist monasteries often housed large libraries of scriptures and became important centers of learning.

Within four centuries after Gautama Buddha's death, Buddhism had spread widely throughout the Indian subcontinent, and also through Pakistan and Afghanistan into Central Asia. From there it reached China in the first century A.D. During this period of expansion, Buddhism also divided into two main forms: Theravada Buddhism, which stressed individual attainment of enlightenment, and Mahayana (Greater Vehicle) Buddhism, in which saints, called Bodhisattvas, aided believers in attaining enlightenment. Mahayana Buddhism became dominant in China.

Mahayana Buddhism itself gave rise to a number of sects or denominations. In Pure Land Buddhism, for example, believers called on the Bodhisattva Amitabha who, by an act of grace, would cause them to be reborn into a heavenly paradise, where all souls would await universal salvation. The Chan sect, developed in China in the sixth century A.D., is better known in the West by its Japanese pronunciation, Zen. It stresses the attainment of enlightenment through meditation and rigorous self-discipline. Some martial arts practices are based on Zen Buddhism. Another Mahayana sect, Lamaism, became dominant in Tibet and Mongolia. Practiced within strictly organized communities of monks (lamas), it places great weight on theological studies, and uses chanting, ritual dancing, and the use of sacred images and ritual objects to combat temptation and evil.

Daoism played a role in the development of Chan Buddhism, and Buddhism was soon to influence a reinterpretation of Confucianism itself.

When the prominent Chinese monk Xuanzang visited India at the beginning of the eighth century, he found that Buddhism was already beginning to decline there, in the face of a Hindu revival. Buddhism had become stronger in China than in the land of its origin. But Buddhism was soon to decline in China as well. Toward the end of the Tang Dynasty, Daoist priests and Confucian scholars complained about the economic and political power of the Buddhist monasteries; once again, Buddhism was attacked for its "barbarian" origins. It was said that monks offended their ancestors by refusing to marry and have children, and by shaving their heads—mutilating the bodies that their parents had given them. An official purge of Buddhism in the 840s dealt a severe blow to its wealth and organized structure. At the same time, the minds of China's ruling class were beginning to turn toward a Confucian revival. Buddhism has survived in China, in weakened form, up to the present day. But it never again regained the intellectual prominence, doctrinal purity, or evangelical zeal of its heyday.

Neo-Confucianism

At the end of the eighth century the noted Confucian scholar Han Yu called on his fellow intellectuals to return to a pure, classical Confucianism. He denounced Buddhism as foreign and Daoism as decadent; he complained that the Confucianism of his time consisted of empty rhetoric and shallow learning. People paid attention, and over the next four centuries Confucian scholars labored to study the original Confucian classics and reinterpret them to suit their own contemporary times.

The vigorous Confucian scholarship of the Song Dynasty (960–1279) produced not only a Confucian revival, but a complete transformation of orthodox belief: Neo-Confucianism. This was the work of generations of scholars; it reached its completion with Zhu Xi (1130–1200). As his contemporary Thomas Aquinas reinterpreted Aristotle for medieval Europe, so also did Zhu Xi reinterpret Confucius for Song China. Neo-Confucianism is a subtle and complex doctrine that had three main effects. First, it recaptured the high ground of intellectual life away from Buddhism and Daoism, and made Confucianism once again the unchallenged basis of elite belief and state policy. Second, it created a new Confucian metaphysics to replace the already ancient Han doctrines of Dong Zhongshu. Third, it gave new emphasis to the spiritual dimensions of Confucianism.

Neo-Confucianism, as a revitalized state ideology, helped to give the Song Dynasty the best motivated, most flexible, and most effective imperial bureaucratic government in Chinese history. Unfortunately, Zhu Xi's interpretations of Confucianism quickly became a new orthodoxy, mechanically studied and repeated by generations of examination candidates for centuries thereafter. Despite later Confucian revivals in the seventeenth century and at the end of the nineteenth century, after the Song Dynasty Neo-Confucianism, for the most part, lost its capacity for innovation.

Neo-Confucian explanations of the nature of the world retained many elements of ancient belief, but (under the influence of Buddhism) reformulated them in a much more systematic and sophisticated way. Form, said Zhu Xi, was eternal and perfect. Form was given concrete physical reality by means of qi (matter-energy), which might be pure or flawed. This gave Neo-Confucianism an explanation of the imperfections of the world and the existence of evil (the result of impure matter-energy), and also a means for overcoming them. Both moral government and moral

individuals could strive to rid the world and themselves of their imperfections, approaching ever more closely to the eternal ideal.

This quest gave Neo-Confucianism its spiritual dimension. The life
of the Neo-Confucian scholar should, said Zhu Xi, be governed by a
relentless investigation into the nature of things, with a view toward
making them better; the investigation of the world should begin with
an investigation of the self. Following the example of Confucius himself,
the Neo-Confucian believer found religious value not so much in salvation in an afterlife as in the full actualization of his human potential in
this life. Introspection as a religious goal of Confucianism was emphasized especially by the Ming Dynasty philosopher Wang Yangming
(1472–1529), who was influenced by Chan Buddhist meditation. His
teachings are summarized in the phrase "Knowledge is the beginning
of conduct; conduct is the completion of knowledge."

A short-lived revival of Neo-Confucianism by some intellectuals in
the seventeenth century attempted to come to grips with two problems:
The fall of the Ming Dynasty in 1644 and the loss of the empire to
"barbarians" (the Manchu rulers of the new Qing Dynasty); and the
introduction of new European ideas by Jesuit missionaries. Inevitably,
however, Chinese scholar-bureaucrats bowed to political reality and
accepted their new rulers; Neo-Confucianism did not prove to be an
effective platform for political dissent. The seeming impossibility of
reconciling traditional Chinese modes of thinking with the new ideas
from the West led, by the eighteenth century, to a new phase of Chinese
isolationism, where the West was ignored as much as possible.

At the end of the nineteenth century, a group of prominent intellectuals led by Kang Youwei and Liang Qichao made one final attempt to use
Neo-Confucianism as the basis for sweeping social and political change.
Arguing that Confucius had been a reformer in his own time, they felt
that Confucian doctrine could provide the foundation for China's mod-

ernization. But the 1898 Reform Movement came too late; Confucianism was soon to be swept from its place at the center of China's intellectual life by waves of revolutionary new ideas from the West.

Christianity and Islam

In 632 a group of Syrian missionaries arrived in Chang'an, the capital of the Tang Dynasty, preaching Nestorianism, an old Middle Eastern form of Christianity. Despite official tolerance of the new religion (and of other western Asian faiths, such as Zoroastrianism), the church made few converts. Small Nestorian communities existed in China for several hundred years, but disappeared during the Song Dynasty. Christian missionaries made contact with China again at the end of the thirteenth century, when Rome sent several priests to the court of Kubilai Khan, the Mongol emperor of China. Their aim was both to preach and to enlist Mongol support in the Crusades, but they returned home without accomplishing either goal.

The Jesuit missionary Matteo Ricci arrived in Beijing in 1600, signaling the beginning of a new effort to bring Christianity to China. Initially Ricci and his followers enjoyed some success, both in making converts and in transmitting European philosophical and scientific ideas to China. By the early eighteenth century, however, China was becoming less interested in contacts with the West. Angered by disputes among the various Catholic orders at work in China, the Qianlong Emperor expelled most of the missionaries from the country. The few who were allowed to remain were employed as artists, architects, and scientists, but were not allowed to attempt to make converts.

Christian missionaries resumed their work in China in the 1830s; both Catholic and Protestant missions sprang up all over China. Christian schools, hospitals, and other projects had important effects on the modernization of China, but again few converts were made. With the Communist revolution of 1949, the missionaries were once again forced to leave China. Today only a few million of the more than one billion Chinese are Christians.

Islam also arrived in China during the Tang Dynasty; unlike Christianity, it succeeded in establishing a long-term presence there. By the twelfth century, mosques were to be found in many cities in northern and western China, as well as in the ports along the southeastern coast. They did not become well integrated into Chinese life, however; often the mosques catered less to Chinese converts than to resident communities of Middle Eastern merchants. Of about 35 million Muslims in China today, some 20 million are ethnic Chinese, while the rest are Turkic- or Persian-speaking non-Han people who live mostly in Xinjiang Province.

A tiny Jewish community also became established in Kaifeng during the Song Dynasty and survived there into the twentieth century.

Religion and Philosophy in China Today

Although the rise of Neo-Confucianism caused both Buddhism and Daoism to decline at the elite level in China, both have survived as organized religions up to the present day. On the level of popular belief, however, Buddhism and Daoism tended to blend together without regard for doctrinal purity. At temples where both Buddhist and Daoist images might sit upon the same altar, people presented offerings of incense, fruit, wine, and money and prayed for divine help and guidance. Ancestor worship remained the foundation of popular religion. People maintained ancestral shrines in their homes, mourned their parents for the prescribed twenty-five months, swept the family graves at the spring festival, and held services for the dead in the eighth lunar month. Astrology, fortune-telling, the preparation of good-luck charms, and the use of special techniques to find lucky sites for graves and houses all were part of the rich variety of beliefs and practices that made up Chinese popular religion.

Deep religious belief is not an important part of the lives of most Chinese people today, especially in the People's Republic of China (where religion is tolerated but not encouraged). Traditional religion remains strong in Taiwan, and even on the mainland many people still visit temples, venerate their ancestors, and include in their daily lives a variety of practices that have religious connotations. Religion in China is now primarily a matter of culture more than of faith. If you ask a young Chinese praying in a temple if he believes in the gods, he might reply, "No, but I do this because I am Chinese."

In the early twentieth century, Chinese intellectuals turned their attention to new forms of thinking imported from the West: modern science, democracy, Marxism, economics, and many others. The effort to understand these new doctrines and apply them to China led to what became known as "the battle of the isms." Marxism, with its promises of liberation from Western domination and rapid social and economic progress, won the battle. With the establishment of the People's Republic of China it became the official ideology of mainland China, although it was strongly rejected in Taiwan, Hong Kong, Singapore, and other large Chinese communities outside the mainland itself. Marxism in China was strongly modified by Mao Zedong, who took a Western, urban theory and applied it successfully to making a revolution in rural China.

Marxism has sometimes been described as a "secular religion," and certainly in the last few years of his life Mao Zedong was treated

virtually as a god. But "Marxism-Leninism-Mao Zedong Thought" has not led China smoothly into a modern era of prosperity and social harmony. The struggle to create a Chinese national ideology that is appropriate both to China's cultural heritage and to China's place in the modern world is likely to continue for a long time to come.

Paper image of the God of Fate (Taiwan, 1968), intended to be pasted on the wall of a home in order to bring good fortune. Chinese popular religion today is based on ancestor worship, and incorporates beliefs and practices derived from both Buddhism and Daoism.

Science and Technology

Up until about the middle of the seventeenth century, China was not only the largest and richest country in the world, but also the most technologically advanced. For centuries China was a major exporter of important inventions to the rest of the world. On a purely intellectual level, China also had a rich and ancient tradition of science.

In thinking about premodern China, or indeed any premodern society, it is important to distinguish between science and technology. Science is a mental activity, the systematic application of human intelligence for the purpose of accumulating and testing knowledge. Technology, on the other hand, has practical goals; it is the systematic application of human intelligence for the accomplishment of tasks. We are accustomed to thinking of science and technology as being inextricably linked. And so they are, in the modern world. In premodern societies, however, science and technology often existed in quite separate realms. Science was an intellectual activity, pursued by members of the elite whose main concern was achieving an understanding of the universe and everything in it. Technology was largely pragmatic, practiced by craftsmen. The two could intersect, as when, for example, an astronomer employed artisans to construct equipment to his specifications. Scientific theory was rarely applied to the improvement of technology, however; that depended on trial and error and on accumulated knowledge within a craft tradition.

Modern science—developed in Renaissance Europe, and now universal throughout the modern world—is characterized by the formulation and testing of hypotheses, often by experimental or mathematical means. It is heavily dependent on scientific instruments—technological tools—and in turn has contributed to the systematic improvement of technology. Premodern Chinese science passes none of those tests; neither does the premodern European science of Aristotle, Galen, and Ptolemy. Nevertheless, until premodern Chinese science was dethroned by telescopes, microscopes, and the experimental method, it provided a means for understanding the world around us that was complex and intellectually satisfying, even if it was, by modern standards, untrue.

Foundations of Chinese Science

Chinese science has roots that go back to the oldest levels of Chinese history that we know anything about. Early religious beliefs, observations of the stars and of other natural phenomena, and the attention to climate and the seasons that is natural in any agricultural society all contributed to a basic cultural understanding of the way the world works. For many centuries, however, that knowledge was conveyed in the language of mythology rather than that of philosophy. For example, the observation that the sun's apparent path around the earth is "tilted" —that is, it does not follow the equator—was explained by a myth about two giants. In fighting for the right to rule the universe, they knocked over one of the pillars of heaven, causing the sky to tilt.

During the latter part of the Warring States Period and into the early Han (around 300 to 100 B.C.), a number of Chinese thinkers began to transform this mythic worldview into a systematic science. Their first assumption was that the universe is organic: Everything in it affects everything else. The key to understanding then became finding out how to sort phenomena into categories. Everything in the same category would have similar characteristics; everything in one category would interact in a predictable way with everything in a second category. Interaction at a distance was thought to take place, not by mechanical connections, but through the medium of *qi*. (In Neo-Confucianism that word came to mean "matter-energy"; in earlier Chinese science, it meant something like "resonating force.")

One type of category was dualistic: *yin* and *yang*. These two words originally meant "shady" and "sunny," "cool" and "warm." By extension, they were used to sort things into paired opposites. *Yin* included everything that is moist, earthly, female, and so on; *yang* included everything dry, celestial, male, and so on. A second system of categories was the Five Phases: wood, fire, earth, metal, and water. These were not "elements" in the sense of types of matter that went into making all other materials; instead, they were thought of as five basic categories of substance and behavior. Phenomena of every conceivable kind were correlated with the Five Phases. For example:

Wood	Fire	Earth	Metal	Water
blue	red	yellow	white	black
east	south	center	west	north
Jupiter	Mars	Saturn	Venus	Mercury

There were five flavors, five internal organs, five musical notes (of the pentatonic scale), five kinds of animals (hairy, feathered, scaly, etc.), and so on.

Still another system of categories was tied to the eight trigrams of the *Book of Changes*. (A trigram consists of three lines, which can be either broken or solid. There are eight possible combinations.) The *Book of Changes* was an ancient manual of fortune-telling; its sixty-four hexagrams (each a combination of two trigrams) were basically a random-access index to short texts that gave cryptic advice about the future. But Chinese philosophers from Confucius onward saw the *Book of Changes* as being filled with deep symbolic and mystical meaning. The eight trigrams therefore seemed to early Chinese thinkers a natural way of sorting phenomena into categories of eight qualities.

This type of premodern science, which has been called categorical reasoning, allowed one to say, for example, that something which fell into the categories *yin*, wood, and trigram number one would always interact in a predictable way with something that fell into the categories *yang*, fire, and trigram eight.

The difficulty with this kind of reasoning is that philosophers soon began to assign phenomena to categories in ways that were largely arbitrary and verbal, rather than being based on observation and experiment. There was no sound reason, for example, to select five internal organs as being the key structures of anatomy, and assigning each one to one of the Five Phases. Nevertheless, once the system was established, it at least provided a systematic way of organizing and acting upon knowledge. Chinese medicine, for example, used herbal drugs that were designed to enhance or restrain *yin* or *yang* in one or another of the five organs, in accordance with the influence of each of the four seasons.

The theoretical structure of traditional Chinese science was established by the end of the Former Han Dynasty (first century B.C.). With some later refinements, such as Neo-Confucian ideas on the nature of form and matter, it provided the basis for Chinese understanding of nature for two thousand years, until it was displaced by modern science early in the twentieth century. It was not simply a mental exercise, for it was applied in such fields as astrology, alchemy, and medicine. Its elaborate and somewhat rigid character meant, however, that it tended to be ignored by scientists in such fields as astronomy and mathematics. Developments in those fields came despite, rather than because of, underlying theory.

The Exact Sciences

Astronomy in China developed to a high level of observational and predictive accuracy. Astronomy itself was pursued as an exact science, even though the goal of astronomy—the use to which astronomical knowledge was put—was primarily astrological. It is often said that astronomy is the most ancient of the sciences because early farmers needed an accurate calendar to know when to plant their crops. This is not really so. Agriculture requires only an approximately accurate solar calendar—the kind that could be computed by anyone who stuck a stick upright in the ground and kept track of the changes in the direction and length of its shadow throughout a year. Astronomy has ancient roots, instead, because of the nearly universal ancient belief that what happens in the heavens affects human destiny. An unusual conjunction of planets could signal the rise of a new dynasty; a planet entering a constellation might signal danger to the kingdom "governed" by that constellation; an eclipse might be a warning to a king. The role of ancient astronomers was to make sense of the complex movements of the heavens. Chinese astronomers computed calendars that went far beyond the day-counting needs of agriculture. They also reconciled the lunar year (12 lunar months = 354 days) with the solar year by adding leap months at appropriate times (11 in every 19 years). They predicted the positions of the five visible planets as well as lunar and solar eclipses.

The theory behind such calendars is that predicted phenomena are not dangerous. If you know that an eclipse will take place, appropriate rituals can be conducted to neutralize its bad astrological effects. Unpredicted phenomena, however, were omens. The ruler of China was regarded as playing a pivotal role between heaven and earth. If he maintained harmony on earth, heaven would respond by being predictable and harmonious. Heavenly disorder therefore was a warning of imperial misrule. A Chinese emperor would respond to a comet by writing a formal apology to his ancestors for failing to maintain heavenly harmony, and by declaring an amnesty for prisoners—an act of earthly benevolence designed to win heaven's approval. He might respond to an unpredicted solar eclipse in the same way, and also by executing his royal astronomer for failing to predict it. China's rulers had excellent reasons for supporting astronomy as an exact science; they did not want any surprises in the sky.

By 2000 B.C. Chinese astronomers had defined and named twenty-eight constellations along the sun's apparent path through the stars; by 500 B.C. several hundred individual stars were named. By 200 B.C. the orbital times of the five visible planets were calculated with 99 percent accuracy. In the second century A.D. the great scientist Zhang Heng (inventor of the world's first seismoscope) constructed an armillary sphere—a nest of rings modeling the horizon, the equator, the polar great circle, and the paths of the sun and moon. In the eighth century the Buddhist astronomer-monk Yixing used measurements of shadow lengths—the same method used by the Greek Eretosthenes several centuries earlier—to calculate the circumference of the earth with surprising accuracy.

Chinese astronomy made steady advances through the Tang and Song Dynasties, and reached its high point in the work of Guo Shoujing, astronomer royal to the Mongol emperor Kubilai Khan of the Yuan Dynasty. In the 1270s Guo Shoujing built a new observatory, with instruments that included an armillary sphere driven by water-powered clockwork gears, a 40-foot gnomon (vertical pole) with a horizontal scale to take shadow-length measurements at noon every day, and a massive set of bronze observational rings, six feet across, with finely calibrated scales and sighting tubes. With those instruments, Chinese astronomers came close to the theoretical limit of accuracy for naked-eye observations of the stars.

In the Ming Dynasty, elite interest in the sciences declined, as most educated people devoted themselves to studies of orthodox Neo-Confucianism in preparation for civil-service careers. Meanwhile, science in Europe steadily advanced. When Jesuit missionaries arrived in China at the beginning of the seventeenth century, their astronomy was clearly more accurate than that of the Chinese. At the same time, Chinese astronomers were hampered in understanding the basis for the superiority of European astronomy, for the Jesuit priests were religiously prohibited from teaching the then-heretical views of Copernicus and Galileo.

A Jesuit priest, Adam Schall, was appointed head of the Bureau of Astronomy in 1645; another Jesuit, Ferdinand Verbiest, constructed a set of European-style bronze instruments to replace those of Guo Shou-jing in the imperial observatory in the 1660s. For the next century, the Bureau of Astronomy remained in European hands, and the official Qing Dynasty calendar was calculated by European, not Chinese, methods. The glorious tradition of Chinese astronomy had come to an end.

Mathematics

Chinese mathematics had developed hand in hand with astronomy. By the second century B.C., Chinese mathematicians had devised a general proof of the Pythagorean theorem, but in general, Chinese mathematics was algebraic rather than geometrical; there was to be no Chinese Euclid. A Han Dynasty textbook gave a general method for solving simultaneous equations with two unknowns. By the fifth century A.D., Chinese mathematicians had calculated the value of pi to more than 10 decimal places. Such precision had no practical value, but it was a classic test of computational techniques. Algebra was applied, however, to a wide range of problems, for example in surveying land and in calculating volumes for engineering purposes.

Chinese characters, like Roman numerals, are unsuitable for mathematical calculations; a special system of mathematical notation was devised instead. The abacus, developed from earlier counting rods some time after the Han Dynasty, made pencil-and-paper calculations unnecessary. As a result, when "Arabic" (actually Indian) numerals reached China sometime in the Song Dynasty they had only curiosity value.

Mathematics comes closer than any other science to speaking a universal language; as China's imperial era came to a close in the twentieth century, Chinese mathematicians were able to make a fairly smooth transition from traditional to modern methods.

Alchemy and Medicine

Chinese alchemy, unlike that of Europe, was less devoted to the production of artificial gold than to the formulation of elixirs of immortality. In both cases, however, the goal of alchemy was to understand the nature of time and matter by manipulating materials (usually with heat) and observing their transformations. Alchemy in China was very much an elite intellectual activity; alchemists tried to transform metals from one kind to another using methods that any ordinary metalsmith could have told them would not work. Alchemists succeeded in gaining a great deal of knowledge about the characteristics of materials, but because that knowledge was organized in the framework of categorical reasoning of traditional Chinese scientific theory, it remained firmly bound by false assumptions. Its most famous achievement—apparently a lucky accident—was the discovery of the formula for gunpowder. That discovery was quickly put to practical use; but by the Song Dynasty, most Chinese intellectuals were beginning to lose interest in alchemical studies, which had begun to seem old-fashioned and unproductive.

Chinese medicine, like alchemy, was closely tied to categorical reasoning and systems of correspondence, which provided an inadequate basis for understanding the nature of disease. Traditional Chinese doctors, however, enjoyed the great advantage shared by doctors everywhere: Most diseases go away by themselves. Any medical procedure that does not cause actual harm will thus be regarded as a "cure." When disease did cause chronic illness, disability, or death, medicine could at least provide some physical comfort and psychological support, and a sense that everything possible was being done. Beyond that, Chinese medicine did in fact develop some effective therapies.

Chinese medicine was holistic; its goal was to restore the body to a state of balance, the basis of health. Diagnoses were reached on the

A silk scroll painting from the second century B.C. (redrawn for clarity) showing calesthenic exercises used in military training. Traditional Chinese medicine emphasizes the importance of exercise and controlled breathing for maintaining good health. Exercises similar to these, called taiji, *are still done daily by millions of Chinese.* Courtesy of the Committee on Mawangdui Studies, Institute of Archaeology, Chinese Academy of Sciences.

basis of careful physical examinations, especially of the pulse. Any of several therapies could then be applied. The most famous Chinese technique was acupuncture—the insertion of thin needles at key points on the body, designed to alter the flow of channels of energy. Closely related were techniques of heat therapy and pressure massage. Acupuncture does work, though not for the reasons given in Chinese medical theory. It can provide strong temporary insensitivity to pain, as well as temporary improvement in some nervous diseases. Surgery was not highly developed in Chinese medicine, except for simple procedures like setting broken bones or closing wounds; acupuncture or drug therapies were always preferred.

From ancient times, Chinese medicine relied on a very wide range of herbal and other drugs. The last of a long line of pharmaceutical handbooks, compiled in the late seventeenth century, contains careful descriptions of thousands of medically active substances. The theory on which these substances were mixed to create medicines has no basis in medical science as we now understand it, but many of them undoubtedly worked. Willow bark, for example, contains salicylic acid, the chemical basis of aspirin; foxglove contains digitalis, a potent cardiac drug. Although Western medicine is widely practiced in China today, Chinese medical workers also continue to investigate traditional medicine for effective therapies, often with considerable success.

Acupuncture needles in this woman's ankle, carrying a weak electrical current, provide effective anesthesia as surgeons remove a thyroid tumor from her throat. The patient is awake and alert during the operation.

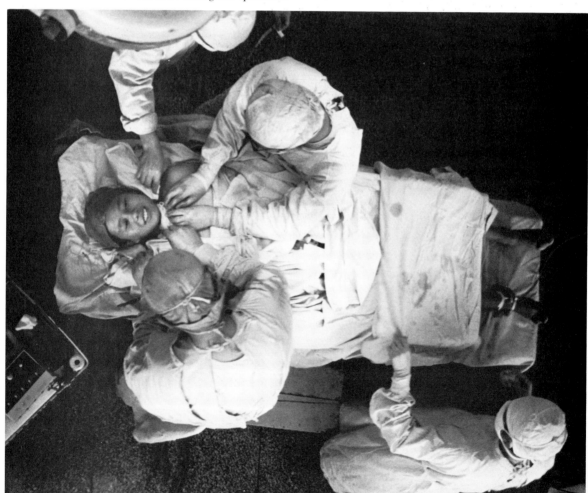

Technology

One of the greatest glories of traditional Chinese civilization was its capacity for inventing and utilizing technology to make work more efficient and productive. This extended over the entire range of human activities.

In engineering, the Chinese developed a wide range of cranes and pulleys to move heavy objects. Mathematically-calculated arches made stone bridges light, strong, and graceful; the oldest extant Chinese bridge has remained in use for fifteen centuries. By the early Zhou Dynasty—1000 B.C., if not earlier—architects were developing the elaborate wooden brackets characteristic of Chinese post-and-beam buildings, spreading the weight of tile roofs over wide, clear spaces. Hydraulic engineers developed a range of techniques for controlling the flow of water, including watergates for irrigation systems, locks (of essentially modern design) for canals, and huge bamboo baskets filled with stone to stabilize the banks of rivers and canals. Techniques to enhance or replace muscle power included the invention of the windmill, water-powered trip-hammers, continuous bucket-and-chain pumps powered by foot treadles, and an efficient harness system that enabled a horse to pull a heavy load without choking. All of these spread from China to the Middle East and Europe. China exported far more technology than it imported, but there were important exceptions to that rule; for example, the noria, a water-propelled pump wheel invented in Syria or Iraq, reached China by the Tang Dynasty.

Transportation technology included not only canals and locks but standardized barges for canal transport. Although China was much more a continental than a maritime nation, Chinese shipbuilding was highly advanced, with particularly great achievements from the twelfth to the fifteenth centuries. In the 1430s imperial fleets sailed as far as

A noria *on the upper Yellow River, Gansu Province. This type of water-propelled irrigation wheel was invented in Syria, and now can be found throughout the Old World, from Spain to Indonesia. It is an excellent example of the transfer of technology in the ancient world.*

East Africa in ships 450 feet long, with multiple masts, sternpost rudders, and watertight internal compartments. They were steered with the aid of magnetic compasses, known in China from at least the early Han Dynasty. On land, the Chinese center-wheeled wheelbarrow enabled a single person to push a heavy load for long distances.

Chinese military technology produced the crossbow (or perhaps borrowed it from the Thai people of southern China, but with great improvements over the original design) by the fourth century B.C. To defend against it, they also devised light, flexible metal-scale armor. The stirrup, which made mounted warfare more effective throughout the ancient world, was possibly a Korean rather than a Chinese invention; it was in use in China by the Han Dynasty.

Gunpowder first blew up in an alchemist's furnace around A.D. 800 and was quickly put to military use. The Chinese developed rather crude mortars and cannon, but rocketry was always their preferred method for launching explosive or incendiary gunpowder bombs. In the thirteenth century Song imperial armies used rockets in rapid-firing racks to slow the Mongol invasions of China. At sea, warships used double-action pumps to spray flaming streams of a mixture of gunpowder and oil at enemy vessels.

Agricultural technology included, by the middle of the Zhou Dynasty (500 B.C.), specialized equipment for constructing and irrigating terraces, as well as efficient iron-tipped plows. Plant breeding became a highly developed art; by around A.D. 1200 Chinese farmers had access to hundreds of varieties of rice selected for special conditions of soil, climate, and length of the growing season. Around the same time, harvested crops (still cut by hand, with sickles) were processed with portable, foot-powered threshing machines and winnowing fans. Some of the crop would be used to brew grain-based wines, with careful control of yeast cultures. Distillation equipment, closely related to that used by alchemists, was used to turn some of the wine into brandy.

Production technologies included metallurgy and ceramics, both of which depended on the control of fire. Zhou Dynasty bronze casters varied their alloys to suit a variety of uses, from ceremonial vessels to weapons to architectural braces and hinges. By 500 B.C. they achieved high enough smelting temperatures to begin to produce cast iron as well. In ceramics, high-fired glazed stoneware was being produced around the same time. By the late Tang Dynasty, control of not only the temperature but also the oxygen content of kilns led to the development of porcelain. During the Song Dynasty, export porcelain—"china"—became famous throughout the Old World.

Salt production depended not only on deep brine wells but also on the use of fire to heat large iron evaporation pans. In Sichuan a deep well was as likely to yield natural gas as it was to produce brine. When that happened, the well was capped and the gas drawn off through bamboo pipelines to provide fuel for the evaporating fires. A picture on a decorated tile from the first century A.D. shows that the whole process was already fully developed by that time.

From Neolithic times onward the Chinese used silk cloth to clothe the rich and hemp-fiber cloth for the less affluent. (Cotton was a late import, reaching China only in the Ming Dynasty.) The complex processes of raising silkworms, boiling and unwinding cocoons, and spinning, dyeing, and weaving silk threads were all mastered early. By the Han Dynasty, Chinese weavers were using foot-powered multiharness looms (and apprentice-powered jacquard looms) to produce luxury fabrics. A treasure trove of silk cloth from a tomb dated 168 B.C. shows that virtually every type of woven cloth known today, from gauze to damask to brocade, was already being produced during the Han.

Along with gunpowder and the compass, paper and printing are the most famous of China's gifts to the world. During the Zhou Dynasty, documents were written on rolls of silk, or, for ordinary purposes, thin strips of wood bound into rolls. Paper was invented by 200 B.C., but it took several centuries to perfect the technology of mass-producing good quality paper from mulberry bark or hemp. By 200 A.D., paper came into widespread use, not only for writing and painting, but for lanterns, umbrellas, and fans. In the thirteenth century Marco Polo was astonished at the sight of paper money.

A bamboo rocket being fired from a platform during a festival in southwestern China. Beginning in the eleventh century A.D. rockets of this type were used by Chinese armies to launch explosive or incendiary warheads.

The idea for the invention of printing in China came from two sources: The first was the use of paper and ink to make rubbings of stone inscriptions; the second was the use of inked seals for signatures on official documents. No one knows exactly when printing itself was invented, but it was closely associated with the rise of Buddhism as a popular religion in China. Buddhist believers liked to carry verses from the scriptures with them or keep them in their homes; the need to produce them in massive quantities probably led to the development of wood-block printing by around 600 A.D. The first printing blocks were hardly more than large seals, with Chinese characters carved in mirror-image form onto the surface of the block. Buddhist temples also needed multiple copies of entire scriptures, however, and by 800 A.D. block printing of whole pages at a time began to satisfy that need, replacing mass-production hand copying by monks.

During the eighth century, the Tang emperors sponsored a project to carve the entire text of the official Confucian classics on hundreds of stone tablets, so that candidates for the civil service examinations could make rubbings from the stones. By the Song Dynasty, in the tenth century, that was no longer necessary; the Confucian classics, along with books of every other type, were printed in wood-block editions. At the same time, books bound with string and enclosed in cardboard wrappers replaced rolled scrolls or accordion-folded booklets.

Movable type was invented during the Song Dynasty and perfected in Korea during the early fifteenth century. Many Chinese books continued to be printed from wood blocks rather than from set type, however. The work of sorting, storing, and re-setting a type font that might include several thousand different characters was time-consuming and demanded great skill. It was often easier to employ workers to carve new double-page blocks for each new edition.

How, or even whether, the invention of printing traveled from China to Europe is a great mystery. Chinese printed works were certainly known in both India and the Arab world. It is reasonable to assume that some European traveler returned from the Middle East or Central Asia to transmit (as Marco Polo had not done, in any detail) the idea of printing with movable type. If you know that something has been done, it is often not too difficult to figure out how to do it again—to reinvent a process on the basis of the product. Very likely Gutenberg did just that, though how he got the idea is still unknown.

China's Scientific Legacy

Many people have wondered why China, with its rich heritage of science and technology, has never produced a scientific revolution. In a sense, that is the wrong question. China followed the usual pattern of premodern scientific traditions—a theoretical dead end accompanied by continuing technological advancement. Europe alone, of all the world's scientific traditions, gave rise to a scientific revolution; this exception to the rule is what really requires explanation. Still, some comparisons are useful.

Scientists and engineers were never more than a small fraction of China's intellectual elite. For most people, an official career was the safe route to wealth, power, and status. Intellectual conversation tended to center on history, philosophy, and literature rather than science or mathematics. Moreover, scientists, with Chinese respect for the past, saw themselves as working in a tradition of knowledge extending back to some classic text or great thinker—a symbolic ancestor. Innovation was often valued, but revolutionary departures from respected traditions were not. Most intellectuals were content with their understanding of the universe and felt no incentive to inquire further.

In addition, Chinese technology was generally adequate, and even progressive, within the structure of traditional Chinese society. Militarily secure, China seldom was caught in a European-style arms race that might produce radical scientific and technological spinoffs. (Galileo was a military engineer as well as an astronomer, for example.) China felt little of the commercial competition that acted as an engine to drive European invention in many fields. Moreover, very few members of China's ruling class took an interest in applied technology. Porcelain workers achieved a sophisticated control of kiln gasses in practice, but they had no idea what oxygen was. No Chinese Priestley or Lavoisier undertook to devise the experiments needed to find out.

Within China's prosperous and technologically advanced society, certain kinds of activities that in Europe played a role in the scientific revolution seemed, instead, a waste of time. From the tenth through the thirteenth centuries Chinese astronomers and instrument makers built a series of elaborate water-powered clocks for imperial palaces, with bells, drums, and puppets to announce the hours. But they were really just showpieces, expensive toys, that did not lead to the widespread use of clocks in society; sundials were cheaper and more accurate. No tradition of experimental science existed in China to drive the search for ever-more-accurate mechanical measurement of time. Again, the magnificent Ming fleets and their voyages of exploration were opposed by many high officials as an expensive exercise in imperial vanity, unlikely to produce useful results. Tiny Portuguese ships, rather than huge Chinese ones, conquered the South Seas to found commercial empires.

When a new, revolutionary generation of Chinese intellectuals arose at the beginning of the twentieth century, one of their top priorities was to dump the entire heritage of premodern science and technology and to adopt Western methods as rapidly as possible. Only in recent years, and largely inspired by the work of Western historians, have the Chinese begun to look back with pride on the magnificent achievements of their own scientific and technological past.

Art and Literature

As was true everywhere in the premodern world, Chinese art and literature was associated primarily with the ruling elite. But at various levels, the arts pervaded traditional Chinese culture. Bronze vessels and jade ornaments, paintings on silk and fine ceramics, were the possessions of the wealthy and powerful; but ordinary people were exposed to sculpture and religious paintings in temples, and many objects of daily use were beautiful as well as functional. Poetry and classical literature were enjoyed by the elite, as folk songs, storytellers' tales, and popular theater were by commoners.

For most of Chinese history, artists were anonymous craftsmen, making things of luxury and beauty for the ruling class. In ancient times scholars were often writers and amateur musicians; the ideal of the scholar-gentleman as poet, calligrapher, painter, and connoisseur of all the arts developed only gradually, reaching its full flowering in the Song Dynasty and beyond. Every period of Chinese history produced things of beauty; all the arts underwent dynamic evolution over time.

The Plastic Arts

The earliest Chinese works of art—or, at least, the only ones that survive from antiquity—were made of solid, three-dimensional materials. Of those, works in bronze are the most dramatic and highly refined. For the rulers of the Shang Dynasty (1576–1059 B.C.), bronze vessels were an indispensable part of religious rituals and funeral rites. The shapes of the vessels were prescribed by ritual requirements (specific shapes were required for containers for sacrifices of grain, meat, and wine, for example). The surface decorations cast into the bronze itself presumably had powerful (though now obscure) religious significance. Bronze vessels, in other words, were not made simply to be objects of beauty; they were nevertheless very beautiful. The Chinese technique of casting bronze involved making a ceramic model, making a ceramic cast of the model, assembling the cast in sections to serve as a mold, and finally pouring molten bronze into the mold. On a purely technical level, the workmanship of the finest Shang bronzes has never been surpassed, anywhere in the world.

Both the shapes and the decoration of bronze vessels changed after the Shang Dynasty, throughout the Zhou and into the Han. From the Han Dynasty (206 B.C.–A.D. 220) onward, bronze vessels declined in ritual importance, and correspondingly declined in their aesthetic quality. With the introduction of Buddhism into China, bronze was often used to make religious statues and other Buddhist ritual objects. Shang bronzes were highly prized by collectors of antiquities in the Song

Dynasty (A.D. 960–1279), but by that time bronze-casting itself had declined to the status of a minor art.

Just as bronzes were buried in the tombs of the wealthy, Chinese sculpture originated in association with funeral rites. As human sacrifice was abandoned during the Zhou period, figurines of wood or clay took the place, symbolically, of sacrificial victims. The more than six thousand larger-than-life-size soldiers made for the First Emperor of Qin around 210 B.C. comprised the largest and most spectacular of ancient China's underground armies, but by no means the only one. The Han general Huo Qubing, for example, was buried with almost two thousand clay soldiers about twenty inches tall. Han tombs were often filled with clay models of animals, chariots, and even houses, providing a vivid image of the life of that time.

Tomb figurines reached their highest point of development during the Tang Dynasty (A.D. 618–907). Tens of thousands of beautiful small sculptures of people, horses, and camels have been recovered from Tang tombs all over China. They often were decorated with colored glazes. The figurines are so lifelike that they can be used to trace changes in fashion, decade by decade, throughout the Tang. After the Tang, however, tomb figures tended gradually to become cheaper, cruder, and less appealing.

Stone sculpture also was associated with tombs. The underground stone chambers of many Han tombs were decorated with complex and beautiful relief sculptures. Monumental figures, sculpted in the round, of fierce mythical beasts were placed near the tombs as guardians. From the Tang Dynasty onward royal tombs were always approached by long

Ceremonial wine container used in royal ancestral sacrifices, Shang Dynasty, ca. 1200 B.C. This vessel typifies both the beauty and the craftsmanship of early Chinese bronzes. Courtesy of the Freer Gallery of Art, Smithsonian Institution, Washington, D.C.

avenues lined on both sides with huge stone figures representing animals, soldiers, and officials. Those at the Ming Tombs near Beijing are only the most famous of many such sculptures.

Sculpture also became closely associated with Buddhism, as images of Buddhas and saints became objects of devotion. The earliest examples, from the Northern Wei Dynasty (A.D. 386–534) are stiff, formal, and monumental, clearly derived from Han stone reliefs. By the Tang, Buddhist sculpture became more graceful and sensual, hinting at the paradise that awaited believers. The typical pose of Tang Buddhist sculptures, with the torso gently curved and one hip thrust to the side, reflects, ultimately, Greek influence. The conquests of Alexander the Great in the fourth century B.C. had planted the seeds of a Hellenic style of sculpture in Afghanistan, where it flourished and eventually spread to Tang China.

Chinese sculpture was rarely separated from some religious or ritual purpose—tomb figures, Buddhist and Daoist religious images—or from some functional quality, as in the case of architectural ornaments. The creation of sculptures solely as works of art was a late and minor development.

As our word *china* suggests, ceramics have always had a place of honor among the plastic arts of the Middle Kingdom. For at least 7000 years the Chinese have made strikingly beautiful objects of clay. Painted pottery from the Neolithic Period remains as appealing to our eyes as it must have been to the people who made and used it. Glazes were discovered during the Shang Dynasty, and clay vessels began to

Tang Dynasty tomb figure depicting a female court musician playing the cymbals. Small scuptures of this sort, of tricolor-glazed earthenware, were not intended to be displayed as works of art; they were funeral offerings buried to accompany the deceased in the afterlife. The Asia Society, New York, Mr. and Mrs. John D. Rockefeller III Collection. Photography by Otto E. Nelson.

be fired at higher temperatures, making them harder and more durable. During the Zhou and Han periods, green-glazed stoneware vessels were often made in shapes that imitated bronze, providing funeral offerings for people who could not afford the real thing. The tricolor glazes that make Tang tomb figurines so beautiful were applied also to plates and cups for the tables of the wealthy; dinnerware of that type was exported to Korea and Japan. During the Tang, potters also developed the stoneware known as celadon (a French term referring to glazes in various shades of green). Celadon was raised to a fine art during the Song Dynasty, which also saw the creation of true, pure-white porcelain.

The Song period produced some of the most elegant ceramics ever made anywhere in the world: vases, bowls, and cups with perfectly balanced shapes and crystal-pure monochrome glazes. Officially supported by the imperial court and patronized not only by the wealthy elite but even by people of modest means, Chinese potters from the Song period onward constantly pushed forward the frontiers of ceramic technology. The Yuan and Ming periods were dominated by blue-and-white porcelain, the Qing by enamel glazes in every color of the rainbow. By the middle of the Qing period (eighteenth century), however, an element of vulgarity began to creep into Chinese ceramics. Many pieces of late imperial porcelain are overdecorated, displaying more technical skill than aesthetic refinement.

Jade carving was also an ancient art in China, with roots in the Neolithic Period. Throughout Chinese history, jade has been admired as a symbol of rectitude—it will break, but it will not bend. Jade is too hard to be carved with metal tools; it must be shaped by abrasion. The

This vase, of Cizhou glazed stoneware, typifies the elegance and sophistication of Song Dynasty ceramics. Vases of this shape were intended specifically to hold a spray of plum blossoms, a flower that symbolized purity and rebirth.   The Asia Society, New York, Mr. and Mrs. John D. Rockefeller III Collection. Photography by Otto E. Nelson.

jade carver's tools were a stretched silk string, bamboo drills, sand, and water. The carving of even the smallest piece of jade was slow and laborious work, demanding great skill. Jade was employed during the Shang and Zhou dynasties and beyond for a variety of symbolic implements used in official rituals, and also for jewelry, belt hooks, and hair ornaments. In later times it was used for a wide range of decorative objects; jade continues to be admired in China as the most beautiful of all stones.

Lacquer, made from the hardened sap of the lac tree, was discovered in the Chang Jiang Valley sometime around the middle of the Zhou Dynasty. As a waterproof and heat-resistant coating for wood it was very useful for making plates, cups, bowls, boxes, and other utensils; such objects often were also very beautiful. Utensils finely decorated in red and black lacquer have emerged from Han Dynasty tombs in perfect condition. In the Ming Dynasty lacquer workers used the technique of laying down hundreds of layers of lacquer on the surface of an object —a process that might take over a year—and then carving the lacquer to produce decoration in deep relief. Ming and early Qing lacquer was admired throughout East Asia and in Europe. From the late sixteenth century onward, however, Japan rather than China has produced the world's finest and most beautiful lacquerware.

Calligraphy and Painting

The development of good-quality, inexpensive paper around 200 A.D. set the stage for the emergence of calligraphy as a fine art. More convenient than slips of wood, less expensive than silk, paper made possible the thousands of hours of practice needed to write Chinese characters beautifully. The high prestige attached to the written word, combined with the aesthetic possibilities of the characters themselves, soon led the Chinese to regard calligraphy as the finest of the fine arts.

Different styles of script were developed, such as a formal hand, cursive script, and a kind of elegant shorthand called "grass writing." Some decorative scripts were based on the archaic characters found on oracle bones or ancient bronze vessels. Every member of the upper class was expected not only to be able to write, but to write well. Excellent calligraphy was taken as evidence on paper of the writer's tranquil self-cultivation and spiritual enlightenment. The best calligraphers of any era became celebrities, and their writings were highly prized as works of art and as models for later generations to follow.

The calligrapher's tools were paper, writing brushes, sticks of dried ink, and a small grindstone on which to mix the ink with water. These, the "four treasures of the scholar's studio," would also become the foundation of Chinese painting in its fully developed form, as artists adapted the brushstrokes and the black-and-white purity of fine writing to produce pictures. Painting had other roots as well, however, and a long period of development leading up to the scroll paintings that came to typify Chinese art.

The earliest surviving Chinese paintings date to the Warring States and early Han periods. Predictably, they have been found in tombs. Some are done in lacquer, on painted boxes or baskets; a very few paintings on silk also are known from that period. Apparently they were carried as banners in a funeral procession, and then buried with the dead. Some Han tombs are decorated with murals depicting scenes of daily life and also of magical animals. Mural painting developed greatly after the Han. The cave-temples at Dunhuang, along the Silk Route in western Gansu Province, are decorated with thousands of square feet of murals dating from about A.D. 400 to 1100, filled with pictures of Buddhas and saints, and scenes from the Buddhist paradise. Some Tang Dynasty royal tombs also were decorated with murals, showing scenes of palace life.

All of these early paintings were done in bright colors, and are filled

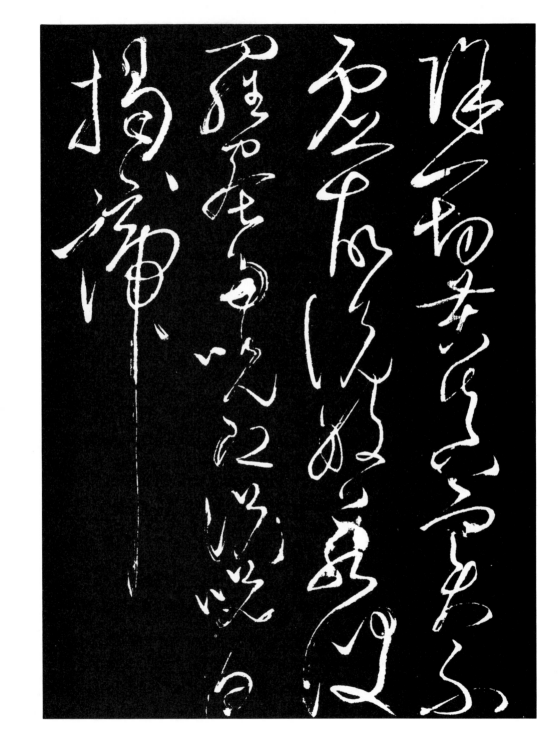

with large figures of deities, people, and animals. A very few paintings on silk from the Tang period also are devoted to representations of the human form. Landscape painting began to appear during the Tang, but only as a background for human subjects. Early in the Northern Song period, however—around the eleventh century A.D.—a revolution in Chinese painting occurred, as artists began to paint pure landscapes in which people appeared only as tiny figures dominated by their surroundings.

The landscape paintings of the Northern Song established conventions of visual art that remained dominant in China for a thousand years, and that continue to live in the paintings of contemporary artists who work in the traditional style. Chinese artists adopted a perspective that is not fixed in time and space; shadowing is unimportant or absent, and ground planes do not converge to a single point. These qualities give Chinese landscape paintings an air of mystery and eternity. Water-based inks (both black and colored) are used exclusively. The earliest landscape paintings were usually done on silk; later artists employed paper as well. In either case, the paintings were mounted as hanging scrolls, intended to be displayed within the houses of the elite. Unlike Western paintings—in durable oils on wood or canvas, mounted in heavy frames—Chinese scroll paintings were seldom hung for more than a few days at a time.

Different styles of landscape painting quickly developed, each associated with a particular master. Some artists worked exclusively in black ink, producing an ascetic, monochrome effect; others used colors as well, including a glowing blue-green that created a "fairyland" atmo-

Wang Xizhi (A.D. 321–379) was one of the most famous calligraphers in Chinese history. His graceful, fluid script was studied by generations of artists. Writings by famous individuals were often preserved by being carved in precise detail on smooth slabs of stone, from which rubbings like this one could be made.

sphere. The theme of landscape painting itself was received with great enthusiasm by members of the elite. As with calligraphy, its development was linked to the idea of spiritual self-cultivation that had roots in Chan Buddhism and philosophical Daoism, and which gave the Song philosophy of Neo-Confucianism much of its vitality. Contemplating a landscape painting of towering mountains, deep valleys, and mist-filled distances, one only gradually becomes aware of tiny houses and human figures in their midst, symbols of the harmonious blending of human existence into the grander world of nature.

Chinese landscape painting has undergone a great deal of evolution since its beginnings in the Northern Song. Although many later artists continued to work in the monumental style of the early masters, by the Yuan Dynasty others developed a landscape style that seems less mysterious and more intimate in scale. Poems, written in beautiful calligraphy, were often incorporated into the composition of the paintings themselves; works that united the ''three perfections'' of poetry, calligraphy, and painting were much admired.

Prior to the Song, painting had been, with few exceptions, an anonymous, professional activity. Painters were usually craftsmen, not gentlemen. From the Song onward, however, many members of the scholarly elite became painters, and although some of them, in fact, made their living as artists, they always regarded themselves as amateurs, practicing one of the many arts appropriate to a gentleman. Painting in the ''amateur'' scholarly tradition was deeply rooted in calligraphic brushwork, and strongly symbolic in content. Works in this tradition were, of course, admired for their technical and aesthetic qualities, but they were also expected to have philosophical meaning. This applied not only to landscapes but to paintings of many other subjects. Pine trees symbolized long life, for example; bamboo was a symbol of rectitude and loyalty, plum blossoms denoted purity. Cranes also symbolized long life,

The landscape became established as the highest form of Chinese painting during the Northern Song Dynasty (960–1127), and dominated traditional painting thereafter. Zhou Ning, a typical scholar-artist of the eighteenth century, worked within that tradition, depicting humans and dwellings fitting harmoniously into the grandeur of nature. Integrated into this painting's composition is a poem describing the blended colors of mountains and trees as the retired scholar sits in his thatched hut awaiting the arrival of spring.

as well as the ability to make spiritual journeys to higher realms of understanding.

From the Song Dynasty onward the work of professional artists usually had much less prestige than that of scholarly amateurs. Members of the imperial academies of art were exceptions to that rule, as were a few other professionals who became rich and famous. But most paid artists—painters of portraits, religious images, and narrative scrolls—remained craftsmen; their work was considered decorative or functional, but not profound. The same scholarly judgment awaited the work of Jesuit missionary-artists in the seventeenth century. The vivid oil paints and converging-line perspective that they used to show off European cultural attainments were dismissed by Chinese connoisseurs as mere optical tricks that had nothing to do with art. Conversely, Chinese landscape painting was not admired in Europe until the Impressionists began to explore the visual effects of light and atmosphere— an exploration that the Northern Song masters had also undertaken, in a very different way, nearly a thousand years before.

In modern China painting has followed three main trends. First, traditional painting has remained important. Twentieth-century masters of the brush, such as Qi Baishi and Zhang Daqian, have employed classical materials and techniques to create scroll paintings that are traditional in inspiration but modern in expression. This style of painting is widely practiced in China today, both as an amateur pursuit and as a minor handicraft for the export market. The spread of literacy throughout society has also encouraged the development of calligraphy as a hobby. Second, with the strong encouragement of the Chinese Communist Party, many professional artists have devoted themselves to creating poster art in the Russian Socialist-Realist style. Bright colors and lively, upbeat themes prevail over purely aesthetic qualities in this "art for the masses." Third, an explosion of artistic creativity has taken place in China in the liberalized atmosphere since the death of Mao Zedong in 1976. Young Chinese artists are beginning to make their mark on the international art scene with works in traditional materials, Western oils, and a variety of contemporary techniques, in styles ranging from photorealism to abstraction.

An elderly scholar burns incense in front of an ancient tree; his page boy stands by, holding a lute in a case. Although Chinese painting was in a state of decline by the late Qing Dynasty, a few artists, such as Ren Bonian (1840–1896), continued to produce works of high quality. The gently satirical tone of this painting, done in a traditional caricature style, shows that at least some scholar-artists were capable of viewing the pretensions of the elite class with a sense of humor.

林下香語天
光緒乙酉二月伯年

Architecture and Gardens

Ordinary Chinese houses and other small buildings are typically made of brick, with roofs of tile supported on a wooden framework. They are often quite plain, except for windows of ornamental grillwork. Larger buildings, such as mansions and palaces, temples, and other ceremonial structures, are almost always of post-and-beam construction. Strong wooden pillars support the roof, the weight of which is distributed by elaborate brackets. Walls enclose space but support no weight. Chinese architects have taken advantage of this type of construction to design buildings that are beautiful as well as sturdy. Pillars and brackets are often brightly painted, leading the eye upward to the roof line. Roofs extend well beyond the walls on all sides and, especially in southern China, are often swept up at the ends in graceful curves. Because walls do not carry any load, they can be pierced by large wooden double doors and latticework windows.

Except for the smallest houses, Chinese buildings are usually surrounded by walls that enclose courtyards. The main gate of a compound always opens to the south, and buildings are built against the northern wall. Larger compounds might include several courtyards arranged symmetrically along a north-south axis. Towns and cities were built on a grid plan and surrounded by walls. The most important official buildings—in a town, the magistrate's office; in a capital city, the emperor's palace—were built adjoining the center of the northern wall. From its entrance, a main street ran to the south gate of the city; another main street intersected it, connecting the eastern and western gates. The overall impression was of a nest of boxes: houses and courtyards, blocks, quarters, and finally the city itself—their symmetry a reflection of the orderly universe. The seat of government overlooked it all from the north, as the pole star dominates the sky.

From The Classic of Poetry

Wang lu tan tan	The king's army, innumerable,
Ru fei, ru han	As if flying, as if soaring,
Ru Jiang, ru Han	Like the Chang Jiang, like the Han,
Ru shan zhi pao	Like a mountain's firmness,
Ru chuan zhi liu	Like the flow of a stream,
Mian mian yi yi	Columns and flanks,
Bu ci bu ke	Unmeasurable, indomitable,
Zhuo zheng Xu guo	Mightily swept through the Kingdom of Xu.

This verse from a longer poem entitled "Forever Martial" tells of a war fought by King Xuan of the Zhou Dynasty (reigned 827–781 B.C.) to conquer the Kingdom of Xu, in the Huai River Valley. The four-word lines capture well the compact but highly expressive quality of early Classical Chinese.

From as early as the Zhou Dynasty, poets praised the beautiful parks that surrounded royal palaces; in every era, gardens were an indispensable element of Chinese architecture. From the Song Dynasty onward gardening developed into a fine art. Influenced by landscape painting and by the "amateur ideal" of the gentleman-scholar, gardens became miniature universes within the confines of a walled compound. Abstract in design (though carefully planned), gardens provided relief from the strict angularity of urban planning. Large, strikingly-shaped rocks and plantings of evergreens represented mountains; streams and pools symbolized rivers and lakes. Plantings of azaleas, camelias, bamboo, flowering plums, and other auspicious plants had symbolic as well as decorative value. Small pavilions were placed so that their doors and windows framed landscaped views as carefully planned as any painting. Within such a garden, a gentleman could see himself as he most wanted to be: a responsible official taking a break from the cares of the world, a scholar, a poet, an artist, a connoisseur of all that is fine and beautiful.

Literature

The first two books in Chinese history were the *Classic of Documents* and the *Classic of Poetry*, both compiled during the eighth century B.C. The former is a collection of historical documents from the age of the mythical sage-kings down to the early years of the Zhou Dynasty. Some of them may have been handed down orally for centuries before they were written down; some of them might be simply late inventions, someone's idea of what the sage-kings should have said and done. The *Classic of Poetry* is a collection of 300 ancient poems, ranging in style from formal hymns for royal ancestors to simple folk songs. Both of these works had enormous prestige throughout Chinese history; they helped to define what the ruling elite meant by literature. Scholars were expected to confine their interest to serious literature—history and philosophy for their formality and content, poetry as the highest expression of the beauty of language and as a vehicle for lofty sentiments.

Prose literature, in the elite tradition, meant first of all the Confucian classics—thirteen ancient works that formed the framework of orthodox Confucianism, along with numerous commentaries on those classics. Next came other philosophical works, including those of non-Confucian traditions. History formed the third great category of prose literature, along with nonfiction essays on a wide variety of subjects. Fiction was supposed to be beneath the notice of a serious literary man. Qualities that were admired in prose were a formal, regular sentence structure, elegantly phrased reasoning, and a wide range of vocabulary. Fidelity to the style of the best classical writers was far more highly valued than stylistic innovation. Prose literature was very conservative; a book on any subject was expected to refer often to older works in the same field. A prose essay written in 1800 A.D. is recognizably different from one written a thousand years earlier, but they are also recognizably part of a continuous literary tradition, in both language and style.

In comparison, poetry evolved far more over the centuries, just as it allowed writers more scope for individual expression. Poetry was disciplined literature, written in prescribed metric forms; the forms most in favor changed from age to age, as some began to seem archaic and new ones were created. Many poems were intended to be sung, to the accompaniment of a zither or lute. Almost all Chinese poetry is lyrical, rather than epic or narrative. Chinese literature contains nothing that resembles the works of Homer or the sagas of the Norse and Irish traditions.

After the *Classic of Poetry* the second great collection of Chinese poems was the *Odes of Chu*, which originated in the southern state of Chu around 300 B.C. The poems were mostly literary treatments of religious themes, using rich and ornate language to describe a spirit journey in the company of a god or goddess. During the Han Dynasty, poems in the Chu style gave rise to a genre of similarly ornate secular poetry that described palaces, banquets, and royal processions in an elaborately flowery style. Han poets also wrote much simpler verse that, looking back to the *Classic of Poetry*, imitated the naïve quality of folk songs.

Poets of the Period of Disunion, such as Tao Qian, were the inventors of a new style of poetry that in the Tang Dynasty was to give rise to some of the greatest verse ever written in Chinese. Poetry of this period employed lines of five or seven words each and parallel grammatical

"Moonlit Night," by Du Fu

Jin ye Fuzhou yue,	There is moonlight tonight in Fuzhou—
Guizhong zhi du kan.	My wife must watch it alone.
Yao lian xiao er nu,	Afar I think of my small children,
Wei jie yi Chang'an.	Too young to know about Chang'an.
Xiang wu yun huan shi,	Her billowing hair dampens with perfumed mist,
Qing hui yu bi han.	Her arms of clear jade grow cold.
He shi yi xu huang	When again will we gaze through parted curtains
Shuang zhao lei hen gan?	Together, letting moonbeams dry our tears?

Du Fu wrote this poem in 756, while he was a prisoner of the rebels who had taken over the imperial capital at Chang'an. His family was safe but far away, in the small city of Fuzhou. The melancholy feeling of this poem is characteristic of Du Fu. He conveys a sense of loss, not only for his own domestic pleasures, but for the era of peace that made private pleasures possible.

structure from each line to the next. That simple but formal style, in the hands of poets of genius, provided enough scope to express feelings on every subject from the quiet pleasures of friendship to the sorrows of a nation at war. Poetry became a social as well as a literary activity; scholars corresponded in verse, and every gentleman was expected to be able to compose a poem on whatever situation he found himself in, on a moment's notice. No gathering of Tang intellectuals was complete without poetic games, as each person present had to add a line in turn to a poem composed on the spot. Failure to do so within the prescribed time limit was penalized by drinking a cup of wine. As intended, everyone ended the evening happily drunk.

Many later poets continued to compose works in the Tang style. By the Song Dynasty, however, a new style of verse became dominant; it was freer in structure than Tang poetry, though no less expressive and beautiful. The greatest poet of the Song, Su Shi, personified the ideal of the scholar-official; he was a high and powerful member of the imperial administration, as well as a distinguished man of letters.

After the Song Dynasty, Chinese poetry went into a long, slow decline. Poetry continued to be highly valued, and some very good verse continued to be written. But many people felt that poetry had reached a state of perfection during the Tang and Song periods, and devoted themselves to imitating the models of those eras rather than finding voices of their own. Interestingly, the last great poet in the Song style was Mao Zedong, whose youthful poems in praise of the revolution would have been completely recognizable in style, though not in subject matter, to Su Shi.

Chinese fiction has its roots in the fairy tales, ghost stories, and tales of ancient kings and battles recited by illiterate entertainers at fairs and marketplaces. As early as the Tang Dynasty, such oral tales captured the imagination of literary men, who wrote them down in more formal language and circulated them for the entertainment of their friends. Tales of miracles told by Buddhist priests were another source of popular prose literature. Novels, as such, were a late development in Chinese literature because of the scholarly prejudice against fiction. One of the earliest was compiled in the early Ming Dynasty from earlier oral and written sources. Called *The Journey to the West*, it tells of a Buddhist pilgrim aided on his journey by the magical Monkey King. Novels never quite became "respectable," but during the Ming and Qing Dynasties they were nevertheless widely read. The greatest Chinese novel, *The Dream of the Red Chamber*, was written by Cao Xueqin in the early eighteenth century; it tells of the decline of a great noble family.

Like fiction, Chinese theater was supposed to be too frivolous for members of the scholarly elite, but it was actually very popular with people of all classes. Troupes of traveling players performed in Chinese marketplaces from ancient times, but theater really blossomed as a literary art from the thirteenth century onward. Singing their lines to an orchestral accompaniment, richly dressed actors—female roles were played by men—used a vocabulary of gestures in place of props, fought acrobatic battles, and acted out tales of thwarted love and military heroism. Beijing opera, and a number of other regional theatrical styles, remain living arts today, widely enjoyed and appreciated. Hundreds of plays form the theatrical repertory, many of them written by failed examination candidates of the Ming and Qing Dynasties who made a precarious living at the margins of the literary world.

Modern Literature

Until the twentieth century, all Chinese nonfiction prose was written in Classical Chinese, a formal literary language that, like Latin in the West, was written but not spoken for many centuries. Formal written Chinese must have seemed old-fashioned in comparison with ordinary speech even in the Han Dynasty; by the Qing Dynasty, it was as different from spoken Chinese as the English of Chaucer is from our own. Ming and Qing fiction adopted a more popular form—Shakespeare rather than Chaucer, and with vernacular dialogue—but written Chinese remained essentially a literary language.

Early in the twentieth century, when the intellectual radicals of the May Fourth Movement sought to sweep away the accumulated weight of China's past in order to make China modern and strong, one of their methods was to create a new written language for the modern age. Chinese characters themselves did not change, but they were used in ways that reflected the vocabulary and grammar of ordinary speech in place of the purely literary classical language. Language reform was an instant success in nonfiction writing, in books, magazines, and newspapers; but the creation of successful works of fiction in the new language was harder to achieve. China's first great modern writer, Lu Xun, wrote short stories in the 1920s and '30s that rank with the best twentieth-century writing anywhere, but not many others of his generation approached that achievement. Many of them were hampered first by excessive attention to Western literary models, and later by ideological restrictions on both content and form imposed by the Communist Party. As the children and grandchildren of the May Fourth reformers have emerged onto the literary scene, the short story has continued to be the medium for the best of modern Chinese fiction. Both on the mainland and—especially—in the freer intellectual atmosphere of Taiwan, a number of writers have begun to make full use of the expressive possibilities of modern vernacular Chinese.

The Chinese Revolution

Throughout the nineteenth century, a number of forward-looking Chinese officials saw that China would have to adjust to the rapidly changing modern world. Their slogan—"Enrich the state, strengthen the military"—accurately portrayed what China needed to do to survive in a new era, in which isolation and self-sufficiency were no longer possible. By the time the Qianlong Emperor sent Lord MacCartney's diplomatic mission home empty-handed in 1793, the seeds of both dynastic decline and foreign aggression had been planted. The impact of the West did not cause the downfall of the Qing Dynasty (and with it, the end of the imperial system). But it did change forever China's place in the world, and for a century it distracted the Chinese government from pressing domestic concerns. By the end of the nineteenth century, the call for "wealth and power" had been overshadowed by a more urgent rallying cry: "Save the nation!"

The Opium Trade and the Opium War

European merchants in China in the late eighteenth century, prevented from engaging in the free trade that they sought, took matters into their own hands. Their main weapon was insidious and effective: opium. Opium had long been known in China as a medicine for treating stomach ailments, but the smoking of opium as a recreational drug was introduced from Southeast Asia only in the seventeenth century. The habit, quickly made illegal, remained uncommon for another hundred years. In the late eighteenth century British merchants began supplying Chinese smugglers around Guangzhou with small quantities of opium from India. They quickly realized that they were onto a good thing. By bringing to China a plentiful supply of cheap, high-quality opium, they could earn a great deal of money for their colony in India, and use their profits from opium sales to finance their purchases of tea. As the supply grew, so did demand, and thousands of Chinese became opium addicts.

In 1795 British merchants imported around 1000 cases of opium into China (each case weighed 144 pounds). By 1816, when Lord Amherst visited the imperial court to ask again for the normalization of diplomatic and trade relations (on European terms) and was turned down by the Daoguang Emperor, annual imports of opium exceeded 5000 cases. The opium trade grew alarmingly—20,000 cases by the late 1820s, almost 40,000 in the late 1830s. The government, of course, tried to stop the trade, but its defenses were no match for the smugglers who unloaded the opium from British ships and brought it upriver. And profits from the trade were ample to bribe coast guard officers and civil officials to look the other way.

The balance of trade shifted. China, once a rich exporter of tea, now saw silver flowing out of the country to pay for opium. Tens of thousands of addicts were reduced to poverty and crime by their habits. Far inland, peasants who had never seen a foreigner or an opium pipe also suffered: The price of silver, in which land taxes had to be paid, rose as the metal grew scarce, and so they had to sell a larger portion of their crops to meet their tax payments.

In 1838 the emperor sent one of his most highly trusted officials, Lin Zexu, to Guangzhou with orders to halt the opium trade. When Commissioner Lin's negotiations with the foreign merchants failed, he ordered all the opium in foreign hands seized and burned. The foreigners demanded compensation; Commissioner Lin refused. Hostilities broke out in 1839; after two years of scattered fighting (and constant setbacks for the Chinese), the British began a full-scale military campaign in 1841. Foreign warships and infantry overwhelmed the Chinese. (China, the inventor of gunpowder, was by then centuries behind Europe in the development of modern gunpowder weapons.) As a British fleet sailed northward and threatened the capital, the Qing government sued for peace. In 1842 China signed the first of many "unequal treaties" with the West: the Treaty of Nanjing.

The opium trade was, of course, callous and immoral. Many foreign merchants would have preferred to sell something else to the Chinese. For them opium was simply a necessary expedient to offset the cost of their purchases of Chinese tea, silk, porcelain, and other goods. The Treaty of Nanjing (and similar treaties signed over the next two years with other European nations and the United States) made clear what the foreigners really wanted: free access to China, and free trade. The Canton System of monopoly trade was abolished, and four additional cities (including Shanghai) were opened to foreign trade. Foreigners were allowed to live in the new "treaty ports," and Christian mission-

Commissioner Lin's Letter to Queen Victoria

When Commissioner Lin arrived in Guangzhou with orders to halt the opium trade, he was reluctant to use force until (in proper Confucian fashion) he had exhausted all avenues of diplomacy. In 1839, he sent a personal letter to Queen Victoria asking her to bring the trade to an end.

Your country is very far from China, but still there are barbarian merchants who come here to trade, in order to make a great profit. Why, then, in return for that profit, do they supply the Chinese people with a poisonous drug that does them harm? I have heard that opium smoking is strictly prohibited in your country; that is because its harm is well understood. Since you do not allow opium to injure your own people, why do you allow your subjects to bring it to China? Of all the things that China exports to other countries, there is nothing that is not beneficial. . . .

We have also learned that no opium is produced in the British Isles; only in parts of India under your control has opium been planted. . . . You can surely wipe out the opium plants in those places . . . and cause grain to be planted instead, making sure that anyone who again planted opium would be severely punished. That would be a truly grand policy, one that would increase the public good and eradicate evil. For that, Heaven would support you and the gods would bring you good fortune, prolonging your life and extending your lineage. Everything depends on what you do.

There is no evidence that Commissioner Lin's letter was ever delivered to the queen by her government. Lord Palmerston, the prime minister, refused to listen to any moral arguments against the opium trade.

Paraphrased from the original Chinese text as printed in *Lin Zexu zhuan* (Biography of Lin Zexu), Taipei, 1967.

British troops attack a Chinese town during the Opium War, 1841–42. This engraving by Thomas Allom was based on a sketch by a British officer on the scene. China's defeat by "western barbarians" in the Opium War deeply shocked a nation that for thousands of years had considered itself to be the center of the universe.

aries were allowed back into the interior. Hong Kong was ceded to Great Britain as a Crown Colony. Opium was not even mentioned in the treaties.

The Taiping Rebellion

China's defeat in the Opium War was a profound shock to the ruling class. No one at court could understand how a few odd-looking barbarians, trading at a port in the far south, could challenge the might of the Chinese empire and win. Commoners also lost confidence in the Qing

Dynasty: If the Manchus could not protect the Chinese empire, what good were they? Popular suffering grew, especially in South China, as opium addiction continued unabated (domestic growers gradually supplied more and more of the drug), and the economy was further disrupted. A rapid shift of foreign trade to Shanghai, Ningbo, Amoy, and Fuzhou left thousands of Cantonese boatmen, dockworkers, and commercial workers unemployed.

In striking contrast to the eighteenth-century European enthusiasm for things Chinese, foreigners in China after the Opium War began to regard the country and its people with condescension or even contempt. Tens of thousands of Chinese peasants migrated abroad to work as "coolies" in the mines, canefields, and railroads of the New World, where they encountered severe racial prejudice. These blows to Chinese cultural pride prompted a few people to begin rethinking China's ancient assumptions about the Middle Kingdom's place in the world.

Suffering led rapidly to unrest. A failed examination candidate named Hong Xiuquan, deranged by his failure, had visions (influenced by missionary pamphlets) in which he saw himself as the younger brother of Jesus Christ. Preaching rebellion, he gathered thousands of followers to join him in overthrowing the Qing Dynasty in order to establish the *Taiping Tianguo* (Heavenly Kingdom of Great Peace). His armed uprising began in 1851; by 1853 he had captured Nanjing, and most of the southern half of China was in Taiping hands. Had he pressed his advantage, the Qing Dynasty might well have fallen in the 1850s. Instead he consolidated his power in the south, allowing the Manchus, just barely, to save themselves.

In most respects the Taiping Rebellion was a traditional Chinese rebel movement. It had a charismatic leader and a religious ideology (in this case, a mixture of Christianity and Confucianism). It proclaimed common ownership of land and equal distribution of wealth—elements that are now sometimes seen as forerunners of Communism, but which had also been present in many peasant rebellions in the past. Even its goal of establishing complete equality for women and abolishing foot-binding was not entirely new. In one respect, however, it did inaugurate China's modern revolution. It was genuinely nationalistic, although its nationalism was expressed mainly negatively as an attempt to rid China of Manchus and Europeans.

Ultimately, the Taiping Rebellion was unsuccessful largely because of the incompetence of its leadership and the failure of its ideology to appeal to the Confucian scholar-official class. Losing momentum, it was finally crushed. The inept Manchu Banner Armies were unable to defeat the Taipings in battle after battle. A British officer, Charles Gordon, was employed to aid the imperial forces; his "Ever-Victorious Army" kept the Taipings away from Shanghai, but did not bring about their defeat. Military victory for the Qing Dynasty came mainly through an effective but dangerous expedient. Provincial armies, commanded directly by governors-general, were raised and thrown into the battle. This worked well when the armies were led by loyal officials like Li Hongzhang, Zeng Guofan, and Zuo Zongtang, but in the longer run it encouraged tendencies toward regional fragmentation that were never far below the surface of China's national unity.

By the time Nanjing was recaptured in 1864 and the Taiping Rebellion came to an end, some twenty million people had died as a direct result of the war—in battle, in the random slaughter of civilians, or by starvation from the destruction of crops and fields. But, incredibly, the Taiping Rebellion was only the largest of several Chinese rebellions in the mid-nineteenth century. The empire was also rocked by the Nian Rebellion in Shandong and the North China Plain, by Moslem uprisings in Xinjiang and Yunnan, and secret society rebellions in Shanghai, Amoy, and Guangzhou. China's population, estimated at around 410 million in 1850, had dropped to under 360 million by 1875.

Treaty Ports and Self-Strengthening

In the midst of this appalling destruction, the West began to put pressure on China once again. The Arrow War of 1856–58, between China and Great Britain, was a totally avoidable conflict sparked by a supposed Chinese insult to the British flag, but it provided foreigners with an excuse to win new concessions from the Chinese throne. The Treaty of Tianjin, which ended the war, opened more ports to foreign trade, regularized diplomatic relations between China and the west, placed the collection of Chinese customs duties in Western hands, guaranteed the rights of missionaries, and granted extraterritoriality (the right to be tried in foreign-run courts rather than Chinese courts for crimes committed in China) to all Westerners. When the emperor resisted implementing the treaty, a British army attacked Beijing and burned the imperial summer palace.

This national humiliation led China's rulers, in the 1860s, to conduct a serious self-appraisal; at long last, measures were taken that produced a partial recovery of the dynasty's fortunes. Victorious Chinese generals in the campaigns against various rebellions—men like Li Hongzhang—became national heros. Joined by the brilliant young official Zhang Zhidong, and supported by the able Tongzhi Emperor, who came to the throne in 1862, they proclaimed a new policy of national self-strengthening. An arsenal was built to produce modern weapons, and an Interpreter's College opened to translate Western books into Chinese. Chinese merchants were encouraged by the government to establish modern, Western-style industrial plants and shipping lines. Robert Hart, the Englishman who served as the first Commissioner of Chinese Maritime Customs, proved to be a sympathetic and helpful advisor. Missionary schools, colleges, and hospitals also began to aid in China's modernization.

But the self-strengthening movement proved to be too little, too late.

Chinese entrepreneurs, underfunded and overregulated, could not compete with the foreigners in their treaty-port enclaves. The imperial government, desperately short of cash, could neither support its new policies effectively nor mobilize the bureaucracy behind them. Local officials, demoralized and overburdened, saw little advantage in comprehensive reforms that might threaten their own positions. Zhang Zhidong's own formula for self-strengthening—"Confucian virtue as the basis, Western technology for practical use"—seriously understated the need for fundamental change.

The self-strengthening movement faltered after the death of the Tongzhi Emperor in 1874. He was succeeded by his nephew, the Guangxu Emperor; the new emperor was only a child, and his mother ruled as his regent. The Empress Dowager Cixi succeeded only in presiding over the ruin of her dynasty. Intelligent but not well educated, crafty but not foresighted, self-indulgent and capable of great cruelty, she genuinely wanted to preserve her dynasty but had no idea how to do so. In foreign affairs, for example, she was adept at playing one Western power off against another (the old Chinese policy of "using barbarians to control barbarians"), but she did not hesitate to use funds earmarked for building a modern navy to rebuild the summer palace instead. Surrounded by a corps of eunuchs as loyal as they were corrupt, she terrorized the imperial administration and struck at anyone who threatened her power.

Meanwhile foreign encroachments continued, within China and along its borders. The number of treaty ports steadily increased, and foreigners engaged in a scramble for concessions, trying to control more and more of China's mines, transportation systems, and industry. America, slow to join the scramble but established by 1898 in its newly won colony in the Philippines, proclaimed the "Open Door Policy," designed to preserve equal access for all nations to China's ports. Indochina became a French colony; Russia bit off pieces of China's territory in Siberia east of the Ussuri River and in the Ili River Valley in far western Xinjiang. Most ominously, a new threat arose in Asia itself, with the rise of Japan as a modern imperial power.

War with Japan

Foreigners had been excluded from Japan for 250 years before the American Commodore Perry forced his way into Tokyo Bay in 1853. Responding rapidly to the foreign threat (the Japanese had observed and learned from what was happening in China), a group of young Japanese leaders overthrew the old feudal government and planted the seeds of constitutional monarchy, in the Meiji Restoration of 1868. Within a few years Japan went through a revolution of modernization that made it militarily and economically powerful, ready to challenge the West in the race to acquire colonial control in Asia. Several factors made it much easier for Japan to modernize than it was for China. Japan was ruled by a small military elite (the samurai) who quickly recognized and responded to the threat of Western power. The commoners, conditioned by military rule, were hard-working and used to doing as they were told. Merchants, prohibited by a rigid class system from upward mobility across class lines, had devoted themselves to commerce and become a wealthy, cohesive business community ready to take advantage of new opportunities. After many centuries of cultural borrowing from China, Japan was quick to borrow new ideas from the West with no worries about cultural self-sufficiency. China was huge, ponderous, and tradition bound; Japan was small, flexible, and open to new ideas.

One of the first goals of the new Japanese government was to seize control of Korea. A treaty concluded between Japan and Korea in 1874 without Chinese approval was the first step in prying Korea out of

China's orbit. As Sino-Japanese competition over Korea increased, Li Hongzhang met with the Japanese statesman Ito Hirobumi in 1885 to try to cool down the situation. The Li-Ito Agreement kept the peace for nine more years. In 1894, however, Japan used the excuse of protecting Japanese interests in Korea from a local rebellion to send troops there; the Japanese soon took control of the Korean capital. The king of Korea appealed to China for help; China sent troops and found itself at war with Japan. The Chinese troops were no match for the modernized Japanese army; even worse, all the modern warships that China had managed to acquire were sunk or crippled in a battle with the Japanese fleet. (Through corruption and mismanagement, some of the Chinese ships did not even have the proper shells for their guns.) In 1895, Li Hongzhang went to Japan to sign a peace treaty, agreeing to Korea's being made a Japanese protectorate, giving Taiwan to Japan as a colony, giving Japan special commercial rights in southern Manchuria, and paying millions of dollars to the Japanese treasury to cover Japan's losses during the war. Only pressure from the West kept Japan's demands from being even worse. For China, it was an unprecedented fiasco.

Japan's ambitions did not end with the Sino-Japanese War. It fought and won another war with Russia in 1904–5 over the "right" to control Manchuria. In 1910 Japan annexed Korea as a colony. For the next thirty-five years Japan would try again and again to gain total domination over China.

The 1898 Reform Movement and the Boxer Uprising

China's defeat by Japan (which they called "the land of the eastern dwarfs") caused shock and outrage among intellectuals and common people alike. At the elite level, a group of new young reformers persuaded the Guangxu Emperor to defy his mother and decree a series of sweeping new policies in 1898. Leading the movement was the noted philosopher Kang Youwei. He tried to appeal to conservatives by arguing that Confucius had been a reformer in his own time, and would approve of reform now. His young associate, Liang Qichao, helped to draft proposals for administrative reform, a new educational system, and a planned constitutional convention. The empress dowager struck back quickly, however. She placed the emperor under house arrest and executed the reformers. (A few, including Kang Youwei and Liang Qichao, escaped into exile.) She cancelled the reforms, and tried to pretend that nothing had happened.

In the country at large, however, a new popular rebellion was brewing. The rebels, called Boxers by the foreigners (their secret society was named "The Righteous Harmonious Fists"), had a simple program: Drive the Manchus out of China, and kill all Westerners. The empress dowager, adept at intrigue, persuaded the Boxer leaders to tone down their anti-Manchu slogans and concentrate on the Westerners in China. To impress the West, she appointed Yuan Shikai, the Chinese commander during the Sino-Japanese War (a better politician than he was a general) to take charge of putting down the Boxer Uprising. His secret orders were to suppress the Boxers, but not to suppress them too much.

In the summer of 1900 the Boxers struck. They murdered hundreds of missionaries thoughout China and trapped the foreign diplomatic corps in the embassy quarter of Beijing. Throughout the summer, the world watched as a combined Western army was organized and fought its way to Beijing to lift the siege. The empress dowager fled to Xi'an while the Western troops looted the capital and slaughtered suspected Boxers in the streets. China agreed to pay additional millions of dollars (to be collected from future customs revenues) to the Western powers to cover damages.

The empress dowager died in 1908, having poisoned the emperor—her son—a few days before so that he would not outlive her. By the time of her death, support for the Qing Dynasty had collapsed completely. Only the smallest push would be necessary to topple the new infant emperor from his throne.

The Republican Revolution

Even with all of the calamities that China suffered during the nineteenth century, it took a long time for the imperial bureaucratic system to deteriorate sufficiently to give way to something new. It took a long time, too, for China's elite to recognize that mere reform would not save the nation and to acknowledge that it was time for China to cease trying to be "all under heaven" and accept its place as one nation-state in a world of many. The republican revolutionary movement that finally took the lead in overthrowing the Qing Dynasty is nearly synonymous with one of modern China's greatest figures, Sun Yat-sen.

Sun Yat-sen was born in 1866 into a progressive, well-to-do Cantonese family that despised the Manchus and glorified the achievements of the Taiping Rebellion. At the age of thirteen he was sent to school in the overseas Chinese community in Hawaii; later he studied medicine in Hong Kong, where he also became a Christian. His unusual background and strong sense of patriotism made him keenly aware of China's need to modernize. For a while he supported the self-strengthening movement, but later realized that it would not accomplish its goals. He returned to Hawaii in 1894 and organized a revolutionary

The Empress Dowager Cixi dominated the Qing Dynasty for half a century. Although by the end of her life the dynasty was in a state of near total collapse, she lived in great splendor and expected her every wish to be obeyed. The Bettmann Archive.

secret society among the Chinese agricultural workers there. He never practiced medicine; revolution was to be his life's work.

Dr. Sun spent much of his early career abroad. Hunted by Qing secret agents, he published revolutionary newspapers, raised money in overseas Chinese communities in America and Southeast Asia, and, working with supporters inside China, organized a series of unsuccessful uprisings. He was kidnapped by imperial agents in London in 1896 and was only narrowly saved from being sent back to China for execution; the publicity about his case made him an international celebrity. He established a base in Japan, where he met with other revolutionaries from all over Asia; his United Will Society became a model for other Asian anticolonial organizations.

Meanwhile, back in China, many other revolutionary groups were also at work; Sun Yat-sen made efforts to coordinate their activities. Patriotic merchants formed "rights recovery societies" to buy back, on behalf of China, territorial concessions controlled by foreigners. In a belated reform, the old civil service examinations that had been abolished in 1903 were replaced by a modern curriculum. Many young intellectuals looked to Dr. Sun as a model.

The Revolution of 1911 happened almost by accident. A revolutionary bomb went off in Wuhan ahead of schedule; a riot broke out. Within a few days (foreign-run telegraph offices spread the news quickly) uprisings broke out all over China. The last emperor, still a young boy, was driven from the throne, and China's last dynasty came to an end. Sun Yat-sen was in Colorado at the time, raising funds for the revolution among Chinese mine workers. Hurrying home, he was proclaimed provisional president of the Republic of China in 1912.

After the initial celebrations, grim reality returned. The Republic of China had no money, and foreign banks refused to lend money while it had a "dangerous radical" as president. A familiar figure, Yuan

Shikai, replaced Sun Yat-sen as president, and the organization of the new government got under way. China was a republic, but far from a democracy; its new leaders were elected only by themselves. Even Sun Yat-sen believed that China would need a long period of political education before it was ready for democratic government. The new regime faced many problems, but also enjoyed broad popular support. In addition, it was supported by the nations of the West, in part because a stable China was good for business. But the promise of the young republic quickly faded.

Within a year or two, it was clear that Yuan Shikai himself had imperial ambitions; he was about to announce his own new dynasty when he died in 1916. He was followed by a series of undistinguished presidents who controlled less and less of the country. China disintegrated; military governors of provinces became independent feudal warlords, pillaging the territory under their control and fighting incessantly with one another. When World War I broke out in 1914, both China and Japan declared themselves on the side of the Allies, but Japan acted while China did not. Japan seized the naval bases that Germany had established in Shandong as a treaty concession and so had a military presence on Chinese soil. In 1915, Japan presented the Republic of China with a set of twenty-one demands which, if met, would in effect have ceded Chinese sovereignty to Japan. Again international opinion intervened, and Japan withdrew the worst of the demands; but Japan emerged nevertheless as the dominant foreign power in China.

Meanwhile Sun Yat-sen had left the capital to organize a new revolutionary government in Guangzhou, hoping that next time the promise of 1911 would be fulfilled. He declared his "Three Principles of the People"—nationalism, social welfare, and political rights—and appealed for foreign support. Little was forthcoming. China became widely known in the West as "the sick man of Asia."

The May Fourth Movement

On May 2, 1919, news reached Beijing that the Treaty of Versailles (which ended World War I) contained an international agreement to transfer to Japan all of Germany's former concessions in China. Two days later thousands of students demonstrated on the streets of Beijing and other large cities, denouncing the West and their own government for selling out the nation. These demonstrations gave the second phase of the Chinese revolution its name: the May Fourth Movement.

It was a revolution not in the sense of overthrowing a government, but rather in the radical reevaluation of an entire society. The May Fourth students looked at everything about China and found much that needed to be discarded or changed. The movement produced few concrete political results, but it molded the thinking of an entire generation. In a sense the movement began not in 1919 but four years earlier, with the founding of *New Youth* magazine, written in the new prose language of ordinary speech. Dozens of other modern-language magazines soon appeared, galvanizing young intellectuals to rethink their entire attitude toward education and China's heritage. Translations of Western literature and works on philosophy, science, economics, and social theory were avidly read. Doctrines of every sort were debated—what was the difference between capitalism and socialism, they asked, or between British and American democracy? Were Christian missionaries good for China or bad? The success of the Russian Revolution of 1917 inspired a wave of interest in Marxism. Mao Zedong, a young assistant librarian in Beijing, was one of many intellectuals attracted to the works of Karl Marx. Students, merchants, and ordinary workers found themselves talking together about serious issues for the first time ever, in study groups and debating clubs all over China. Young historians took a critical look at China's past; young artists and writers proclaimed the need to create a new culture for China. Western intellectuals like Ber-

The May Fourth Movement and the Transformation of Chinese Culture

Hu Shih (1891–1962) studied at Cornell and Columbia and became known as one of China's leading young intellectuals even before his return home in 1917. He was at the forefront of the language-reform movement and played a key role in the May Fourth generation's reevaluation of China's past. He expressed the views of many of his contemporaries in calling for a Chinese revolution that went far beyond politics:

What is the foundation stone of contemporary Europe which lies so brilliantly before us? It is the gift of revolutions. The term revolution in Europe means a change from the old to the new, which differs absolutely from what we call the change of dynasties. . . . Because of these revolutions there have been rejuvenation and progress. The history of modern Europe is a history of revolution. . . . In China we have undertaken three revolutions. . . . They began well enough, but were never carried to their logical conclusion. The old dirt was not washed away by blood. But the major cause for the prevalence of darkness in China is that . . . revolution . . . has not been carried out by us in the fields of ethics, morality, literature, and the fine arts, which . . . are the sources of our spiritual life. That is why the purely political revolution is incapable of changing our society. The fundamental cause of all these failures lies in the fact that we are afraid of revolution and ignorant of its function in the improvement of civilization.

Hu Shih, unlike many of his friends in the May Fourth Movement, rejected communism as a solution for China's problems. He remained true to the revolutionary vision of Sun Yat-sen and Chiang Kai-shek, and became an intellectual leader of the Nationalist Party.

Adapted by permission of the publishers from *The May Fourth Movement: Intellectual Revolution in Modern China*, Chow Tse-tsung (Cambridge, MA: Harvard University Press, copyright 1963 by The President and Fellows of Harvard College).

trand Russell and John Dewey drew huge audiences on lecture tours of China.

The world did not change overnight, and by the mid-1920s some of the young intellectuals of the May Fourth Movement had grown disillusioned. The hard work of making a revolution in China returned largely to the political arena. Everyone agreed that China had to become modern; the question that remained was how to do it.

Communism and Nationalism

In 1921 a small group of Chinese radicals—including Mao Zedong and Chen Duxiu (the founder of *New Youth*)—met secretly in Shanghai and organized the Chinese Communist Party. They were helped by advisors from the Communist International, the organization used by Lenin, and later Stalin, to ensure that all Communist parties everywhere would take their doctrine, and their orders, from Moscow. Recognizing that the new party was small and weak, the advisors ordered it to join a united front with Sun Yat-sen's Nationalist Party and work to bring that much-larger party leftward. Under the Nationalist umbrella, the Communist Party quickly established a reputation for being the most radical, energetic, and anti-Western of China's revolutionary movements; membership grew rapidly.

Sun Yat-sen died in 1924, and the nation was plunged into mourning. In the ensuing struggle for leadership within the Nationalist Party, a young military officer, Chiang Kai-shek, emerged victorious. Chiang had been sent by Sun Yat-sen to study in Moscow several years earlier. There he learned that he hated Marxism, but he also learned how to organize a one-party state. Sun's loosely run revolutionary coalition was soon turned into a disciplined political force. In 1926 Chiang organized his Northern Expedition, moving from Guangzhou to Nanjing and on to the North China Plain with the Nationalist Army, crushing warlords

Sun Yat-sen, the main organizer of China's 1911 revolution, is regarded as the "Father of the Country" by Chinese of every political persuasion. He is seen here in a moment of relaxation, wearing traditional Chinese dress rather than the quasi-military uniform he often wore in public. The Bettmann Archive.

along the way or forcing them to become his allies. Chiang relied on the Communist Party to do advance work for the campaign, but abruptly turned on his Communist partners in 1927, arresting and executing thousands of party members. As Chiang triumphantly established his capital at Nanjing in 1928, Communist leaders, on Russian advice, organized a series of urban uprisings, all of which were bloodily defeated. Mao, who argued that an urban-based communist revolution was bound to fail, and that Chinese Communism's natural base was among the peasantry, was put on party probation for heresy.

Mao Zedong on Peasant Revolution

In 1927 Mao Zedong returned to his native Hunan Province to investigate the revolutionary potential of the peasantry there. In his report to the Chinese Communist Party, he wrote:

In a very short time, in China's central, southern, and northern provinces, several hundred million peasants will rise like a mighty storm, like a hurricane, a force so swift and violent that no power, however great, will be able to hold it back. They will smash all the trammels that bind them and rush forward along the road to liberation. They will sweep the imperialists, warlords, corrupt officials, local tyrants, and evil gentry into their graves. Every revolutionary party and every revolutionary comrade will be put to the test, to be accepted or rejected as they decide. There are three alternatives: To march at their head and lead them? To trail behind them, gesticulating and criticizing? Or to stand in their way and oppose them? Every Chinese is free to choose, but events will force you to make the choice quickly.

Mao's vision of peasant-based revolution was rejected by the Communist Party leadership at the time. Later events proved Mao correct, however; the Communist victory of 1949 was won in large part by harnessing the revolutionary power of China's peasants.

Adapted from *The Selected Works of Mao Tse-tung, Vol. 1* (Beijing: Foreign Languages Press, 1965), pp. 23-24.

Japan, still seeking to extend its domination of China, grew alarmed at the prospect of a China united under Nationalist rule. In 1928 Japanese troops assassinated Chiang Kai-shek's ally, the military governor of Manchuria Zhang Zuolin. When his son Zhang Xueliang took his place, Japan invaded Manchuria in 1931 and soon turned it into a Japanese puppet state. Chiang Kai-shek, realizing that resistance was hopeless, pulled his troops out of Manchuria without firing a shot. The decision was militarily prudent but politically unwise; it made Chiang look weak and unpatriotic. But nothing would change his conviction that all else had to wait until communism was exterminated in China. The Communist Party, after a series of lethal campaigns, was wiped out everywhere except for a rural stronghold in Jiangxi Province; that was surrounded and under aerial bombardment. The final campaign led, however, not to the extinction of the Chinese Communist Party, but to its rebirth.

In late 1934, about 100,000 communists broke through the Nationalist cordon around Jiangxi and began a winding, 6000-mile retreat: the Long March. Crossing mountains and deserts, fighting battles all along the way, fewer than 10,000 survived a year later to reach a safe haven at Yenan, in northern Shaanxi Province. During the march Mao Zedong was recognized as the party's supreme leader; he was assisted by his chief administrator, Zhou Enlai, and his military chief of staff, Zhu De. The battle-hardened survivors who made it to Yenan became legends in their own time, and formed the nucleus of China's Communist Revolution.

The Communist taunt that Chiang Kai-shek preferred fighting his own countrymen to fighting the Japanese fell on sympathetic ears. In December of 1936 Chiang's ally, the Manchurian "Young Marshal" Zhang Xueliang, lured Chiang to Xi'an and took him prisoner. At gunpoint, Chiang was forced to agree to stop fighting the Communists, and to form a new united front with them to resist further Japanese aggression. The Japanese, again alarmed at the prospect of Chinese unity, moved troops into northern China. Fighting broke out near Beijing in July 1937. Within a few weeks Japan had control of all of the North China Plain and attacked Shanghai. In November Nanjing fell to the Japanese and was subjected to a week of looting and terror. Chiang moved his government and army upriver to Chongqing. Four years before Pearl Harbor, the Asian phase of World War II had begun.

World War II

In an effort to consolidate their military gains, the Japanese set up a puppet Chinese government under one of Chiang's old rivals, Wang Jingwei. It won little popular support; China chose to fight on. In their western stronghold, Chiang's army suffered through air raids and struggled to hold the Japanese at bay, assisted by American volunteer pilots, the "Flying Tigers." In the countryside, corruption and maladministration were the rule; famine was common, and hundreds of thousands of people starved to death.

In Yenan, Mao Zedong put his theories of peasant communism to a practical test. Land was taken from landlords and distributed to those who farmed it. The Red Army was ordered to work alongside the common people to build roads, schools, and hospitals, and soldiers were prohibited on pain of death (perhaps for the first time in Chinese history) from looting, raping, or terrorizing the local population. Mao's theories of guerilla warfare were applied against the Japanese and proved successful. The Communist forces swelled as thousands of people, from left-wing intellectuals, writers, and artists to ordinary citizens eager to fight the Japanese, flocked to Yenan.

When Japan attacked Pearl Harbor in 1941 and America joined the war, the Chinese suddenly found themselves with a powerful ally. American strategy in China called for keeping as many Japanese troops as possible tied down there, preparing the way for an "island-hopping" campaign in the Pacific. American supplies were airlifted from India to Chongqing, but to the frustration of Chiang's American advisor, General Joseph Stilwell, the Nationalists stayed within their lines. Chiang preferred to save his resources for the civil war that he knew would follow once America had defeated Japan. In the north the Communists, with little outside aid, harassed the Japanese with hit-and-run tactics; they won little territory, but much popular support.

With the bombing of Hiroshima and Nagasaki in August 1945, suddenly the war was over. The American forces in China made sure that the Nationalist Army accepted the Japanese surrender in North China and Manchuria, giving Chiang the dominant position in China after the war. American diplomats tried to negotiate a Nationalist-Communist coalition government for all of China; after all, they thought, the war was over. Nothing could have been less true.

Civil War

By the end of 1946, it was clear that a showdown was inevitable. The Nationalists, equipped with American weapons and supplies, hurled whole armies against the Communists, who tended to melt away into the countryside. In the northeast, Communist forces used their proven methods of guerilla warfare and peasant mobilization to isolate Nationalist forces in the cities. It soon became clear that in the battle for the hearts and minds of the Chinese peasantry, the Communists had won. The Nationalists had the guns and the cities, but the Communists had the people. Even in the cities, the situation grew desperate. Ruinous inflation made the government's currency worthless; a wheelbarrow-load of money might buy a small sack of rice. Many Chinese business-men—Chiang's strongest supporters—began to flee the country.

By the end of 1947, the Americans had had enough. Believing that no amount of aid could save the Nationalists, they pulled out and urged foreigners to leave the country. Left to his own devices, Chiang fought on through 1948, but it was a lost cause. In the climactic battle of Huaihai (north of Nanjing) in early 1949, whole divisions of Nationalist troops turned their guns on their officers and deserted to the Communist side. Nationalist tanks were rendered useless by miles of ditches dug by local peasants organized by Communist political workers. When the Communists crossed the Chang Jiang, Nationalist resistance crumbled. City after city fell to the Red Army; Chiang and his forces retreated to Taiwan (which had been recovered from Japan in 1945). On October 1, 1949, Mao Zedong, standing on the Gate of Heavenly Peace in front of Beijing's Forbidden City, proclaimed the founding of the People's Republic of China.

Modern China and the World

In 1949, the Chinese quest to "save the nation" had at last been fulfilled—or so it seemed. The country was unified (although with the Nationalist government installed in Taiwan, the civil war had not ended, at least in principle); the "unequal treaties" had been abolished and foreign domination brought to an end. It was time to turn again to the unfinished business of making China a rich and powerful nation fully integrated into the modern world. For the next quarter of a century, progress toward that goal was erratic. Mao Zedong, one of the greatest revolutionaries in history, proved less able as the leader of a modern nation. Not until after his death would China achieve a clear vision, in practical terms, of how to become modern and strong. Meanwhile, the Nationalist government on Taiwan worked, under very different circumstances, to create an alternative vision of China's road into the modern world.

Consolidation

After its victory in 1949, the Chinese Communist Party moved as quickly as possible to solidify its control over the country. Teams of party workers were sent to the countryside to create, ironically, an agrarian capitalist revolution. Land was seized from landlords and distributed to ordinary farmers in small private lots. "People's courts" were set up to try landlords, local officials, and other formerly privileged people for abuses in the past. It was a time for settling old scores; millions of people (including many Christians) were executed for real or imagined "crimes against the people." In the cities intellectuals, businessmen, and other people of even modest wealth and privilege were shown, sometimes forcibly, that in the new China everyone was supposed to be equal, even if that meant being equally poor. Opium addicts, prostitutes, and petty criminals were rounded up and sent to labor camps for "reeducation." Many more people fled to Hong Kong or Taiwan.

The new government sent a delegation to the United Nations to claim China's seat there, but the United States rallied support for its old ally, Chiang Kai-shek, and U.N. membership was retained by the Nationalists on Taiwan. The Cold War had begun, and America attempted, with considerable success, to contain and isolate China both diplomatically and militarily. Any chance that China's Communist government had of reaching an early understanding with the United States was shattered by the Korean War.

After World War II, Korea was divided into northern and southern zones of Russian and American occupation. The demarkation line quickly hardened into a boundary between two mutually hostile Korean governments, with a Russian-sponsored Communist regime in the north and an American-sponsored republic in the south. In 1950 North Korea

Despite efforts at modernization and mechanization, much of China's work is still performed by human muscle power.

invaded South Korea; a U.N. force (largely American) was organized to push the North Koreans back again. When U.N. troops approached China's border with Korea, the Chinese, after many warnings, entered the war. The U.N. army was pushed back again, and a truce was negotiated in 1953 with the old demarcation line restored. The war solidified American hostility toward "Red China," and virtually all contact between the two countries was suspended for twenty years. Within the United States, Senator Joseph McCarthy raised the cry, "Who lost China?" (as if China had been America's to lose). American scholars and officials who had predicted the Communist victory in China were hounded by Congress for somehow having caused what they had foreseen.

With China partly isolated from the Western world, Hong Kong—still in British hands—began to grow rapidly as the West's main point of contact with the People's Republic. Shanghai, no longer a foreign-controlled, international city, remained a shipping and industrial center, but declined in importance. Hong Kong took up the slack. A flood of refugees from China created severe social problems and overcrowding there, but at the same time gave Hong Kong a huge labor pool, willing to work hard even for low wages and eager to succeed. With a stable colonial government, a superb harbor, and a free-market economy, Hong Kong quickly grew to become a major international city and the main transit point for China's international trade.

Limited in its diplomatic relations largely to the Soviet bloc and the emerging nations of the postcolonial Third World, China turned to its old ally, the Soviet Union, for support. China's leaders were not very happy with Russian aid and advisors, whom China regarded as arrogant and ungenerous. Moscow was determined to retain its leadership in the Communist world, while Mao was equally determined to forge an independent "Chinese path to communism." But given the urgency of rebuilding a nation shattered by decades of war, help from any quarter was welcome.

Building the New Nation

Domestically, China's newly independent farmers were urged to form rural cooperatives, pooling resources for growing and marketing crops. Within a few years these cooperatives were transformed into communes, in which land was returned to common ownership. Comprehensive laws were passed giving women equal rights with men in marriage and divorce, property ownership, and employment. The first Five Year Plan, implemented in 1953, had considerable success in consolidating state ownership of industry and business enterprises, and in raising both output and government revenues. Artists and writers were urged to create new works of "people's art" to rally support for the revolutionary state and to transform the basis of Chinese culture from the elite to the masses.

All power was concentrated in the hands of the Communist Party. The party was ruled by the chairman (Mao Zedong), supported by the Central Committee and a large party bureaucracy. Government administration was handled by a separate organizational structure, headed by the premier (Zhou Enlai) and a system of various ministries, bureaus, and provincial, county, and city governments. Laws were ratified by the National People's Congress, whose members were chosen in elections dominated by the party. The People's Liberation Army was controlled by the Central Military Commission (headed by Zhu De) and a military command structure. But both the civil government and the army were firmly under Party control.

By 1956 Mao was confident enough of his accomplishments to invite public comments and criticism: "Let a hundred flowers bloom," he said; "let a hundred schools of thought contend." But the chairman was shocked by the barrage of criticism that resulted; it was clear that many people, especially intellectuals and members of the old middle class, were not at all satisfied with the progress and direction of the revolution. The Hundred Flowers Movement came to an abrupt end in 1957 with the Anti-Rightist Campaign, a movement that branded tens of thousands of people as "class enemies," sending them to labor camps or placing them under surveillance.

At the same time, Mao quarreled with the Soviet Union and expelled Russian advisors from China. In 1959 rebellion broke out in Tibet, and the Dalai Lama fled to India. Soon afterward, China and India fought a small, inconclusive war over disputed borders. Tensions grew in the

Taiwan Strait that separated Communist and Nationalist China. Russian troops began massing along the Sino-Soviet border and in the Mongolian People's Republic (which was firmly in the Russian camp). The People's Republic of China was on its own, and beleaguered.

In an effort to renew enthusiasm for the revolution and base it more securely on China's "workers, peasants, and soldiers," Mao in 1958 proclaimed the policy of the Great Leap Forward. This was to be a sudden surge of communization and economic progress on all fronts at once. Under Mao's personal direction, peasants were ordered to "plant grain everywhere"; workers were told to create industrial products out of locally available materials. The policy was a dismal disaster. Centrally controlled agriculture ignored thousands of years worth of local farming wisdom, and crops failed in many areas. Famine was widespread. Thousands of acres of land were destroyed by erosion. Goods produced in new small-scale factories (such as backyard steel mills) were often of such poor quality that they could not be used. By the end of 1960 Mao was forced by others in the top party leadership to cancel the new policy and confess its failure.

Mao was allowed to retain his nominal leadership of the party, but in the early years of the 1960s he was kept away from the reins of power. Moderate pragmatists like Zhou Enlai and Liu Shaoqi struggled to get the work of nation building back on track. Mao brooded as he watched radical communism turn into socialist reform and plotted his comeback.

Taiwan: A Separate Path

The Nationalist government and army had arrived in Taiwan in 1948–49 in disarray and to an uncertain welcome. Political agents had prepared the way by rounding up and executing thousands of Taiwanese students suspected of wanting to turn Taiwan into an independent state. The local population, just recovering from the Japanese colonial period, found the Nationalist refugees (around two million of them) an unwanted burden. But Chiang Kai-shek, with enthusiastic American support, quickly began to turn Taiwan into a showplace of Nationalist Chinese success.

Land reform was one of the first orders of business in Taiwan, as it was in the mainland; but where the Communists executed landlords, the Nationalists paid them compensation (with funds supplied by the United States). Many former large landowners used their compensation to become new industrialists. Private industrial capital flowed in from America, and later from Japan as well; soon Taiwan had a thriving economy in both agriculture and industry.

The Nationalist government was, like that of the People's Republic, a one-party state. A tightly organized party, through its Central Committee, controlled both the administration and the military. Under martial law the Taiwan Garrison Command exercised strict control over the population; other political parties were banned. The Nationalist government steadfastly claimed to be the government of all of China, temporarily based in Taiwan; elections to the National Assembly were suspended "because of wartime conditions." Taiwan itself was governed through a separately organized provincial administration. Although the Republic of China and the People's Republic of China were politically similar in many ways, ideologically they were quite different. The Nationalist government promoted a capitalist economy and (except in matters touching on politics and national security) a relatively open society. Daily life on Taiwan was far freer of government interference than was life on the mainland. Tensions remained between mainlanders and Taiwanese, but the latter, largely excluded from high government and military positions, pragmatically devoted themselves to economic development.

With a large, well-equiped army, and backed by a mutual-defense treaty with the United States, Taiwan was secure in its island fortress. An American fleet patrolled the Taiwan Strait, although some suspected that it was there as much to ward off any rash Nationalist attempt to recapture the mainland as it was to stop any Communist attempt to invade Taiwan. By the late 1960s Nationalist slogans about recovering the homeland had become merely patriotic rhetoric. Emphasis shifted to making Nationalist China such a success on Taiwan that the Chinese people on the mainland would eventually reject communism and invite the Nationalists back. Meanwhile, the two sides remained relentlessly hostile, but at a distance. And, after 1966, Chiang watched with undisguised satisfaction as the Communists began tearing themselves apart once again.

The Cultural Revolution

Mao launched his return to power at the end of 1965. Attacking his own party leadership for "capitalist tendencies," bureaucratism, elitism, inefficiency, and loss of revolutionary fervor, he called on China's youth to create a new Long March to revive the revolution. Millions of teenagers, organized into brigades of Red Guards, took the Chairman at his word. "Bombard the headquarters!"—the Red Guards dragged party officials and managers of factories and communes from their offices, and set up revolutionary committees in their places. "Destroy poisonous weeds!"—intellectuals and "capitalist-roaders" were beaten, publicly humiliated, and sent off to the countryside to "learn from the masses." "Sweep away the old to bring forth the new!"—museums and libraries were sacked, temples and historic sites vandalized. By the time the army moved out of its barracks to restore public order in late 1968, the country was reeling.

The Cultural Revolution continued, however, even though its most violent phase had ended. Revolutionary committees were still in charge everywhere, and policies reminiscent of the Great Leap Forward were reintroduced. Revolutionary fervor was to substitute for investment and expertise in creating economic progress. Education was in disarray, as "learning from the masses" replaced learning from books, and admission to universities was based on revolutionary spirit and a working-class family background rather than academic achievement. With the enthusiastic support of Mao's designated successor, Marshal Lin Biao, Chairman Mao was elevated virtually to the status of a god. The "little red book" of his selected quotations was China's new gospel, and everyone was expected to wear a red-and-gold badge bearing the Chairman's portrait. Through it all Mao's oldest comrades tried as best they could to keep a lid on things. Zhou Enlai kept the administration functioning, though he could not prevent the arrest and disgrace of his friends Liu Shaoqi and Deng Xiaoping; Zhu De tried to keep the army from becoming embroiled in politics.

In 1971 Lin Biao, impatient to assume the party chairmanship, attempted a coup against Mao. The plot failed, and Lin apparently died in a plane crash while attempting to flee to Russia. This was followed by a massive campaign to "Criticize Lin Biao; criticize Confucius." (Confucius, a symbol of moderation and tradition, was a not-very-subtle stand-in for Zhou Enlai.) With Mao in failing health, the final phase of the Cultural Revolution was controlled by his wife, Jiang Qing. She and her associates enforced rigid standards of proletarian purity in everything from dress and personal appearance to literature and ballet. Work was disrupted throughout the country by daily study sessions to read and discuss the works of Chairman Mao. Enthusiastic slogans about "socialist transformation" were seen everywhere, while the country stagnated.

A rally to "Criticize Lin Biao; criticize Confucius," Beijing, 1973. During the Cultural Revolution, Mao Zedong tried to harness the enthusiasm of mass political campaigns to produce "socialist transformation" in China without relying on either traditional elites or foreign technology.

Nixon in China

By 1968 Mao had begun to worry seriously about China's foreign relations. The Russian invasion of Czechoslovakia that reestablished Moscow's control after a liberalization movement there in 1968 made Mao wonder if Russia might attack independent-minded Communist China as well. Border skirmishes between Chinese and Russian soldiers along the Ussuri River and in Xinjiang increased those fears; air-raid shelters were dug all over the country. The Vietnam War was raging, and American bombers flew uncomfortably close to China on their way

The Cult of Mao Zedong

During the Cultural Revolution, Mao Zedong was the focus of an exaggerated cult of personality, and Mao Zedong Thought was taken as an absolute standard of truth. Pictures and statues of Mao were everywhere, and nearly everyone wore a Mao badge and carried a copy of Mao's Selected Quotations. Over and over again, loudspeakers in public places throughout the mainland blared forth the song "Sailing the Seas Depends on the Helmsman":

> *Sailing the seas depends on the helmsman,*
> *To grow, all living things depend on the sun;*
> *Rain and dew nourish the young plants,*
> *In making revolution we rely on Mao Zedong Thought!*
> *Fish cannot depart from the water,*
> *Melons cannot depart from the seed-beds;*
> *In revolution, the masses cannot depart from the*
>   *Communist Party;*
> *Mao Zedong Thought is a sun that never sets!*

to North Vietnam. Both China and Russia supported North Vietnam against South Vietnam and the United States, but it was clear that Hanoi was tilting toward Moscow, threatening to create an unfriendly Russian presence on China's southeastern border. Mao concluded that less-hostile relations with America would provide him with some insurance against the Soviet Union; meanwhile, in the United States, the feeling was slowly growing that it was time to take a friendlier attitude toward China.

President Richard Nixon and Premier Zhou Enlai drink a toast during Mr. Nixon's visit to China. UPI/Bettmann Newsphotos.

In 1971, as a gesture of friendship, an American Ping-Pong team was invited to tour China. With the quiet support of the United States, the People's Republic of China replaced Taiwan in the United Nations in the fall of that same year. Meanwhile, U.S. Secretary of State Henry Kissinger made a secret trip to Beijing to meet with Mao and Zhou. As agreed at that meeting, President Richard Nixon visited China in February 1972. While the whole world watched, fascinated, on television, the long-standing hostility between the United States and the People's Republic of China was ended. The Shanghai Communiqué that summarized the results of Nixon's visit was in part an agreement to disagree, particularly about the status of America's relations with Taiwan. But it did provide for the resumption of trade and for cultural exchanges; each nation soon set up a liaison office in the other's capital. As Chairman Mao said in 1971, "I do not expect the United States to . . . become

· 230 ·

a Buddha; but if the United States wishes to be a realist, I shall be a realist too." For both sides, realism—prompted by fears of Russia— meant that it was time to become friends.

Taiwan was shocked by America's abrupt change of policy, although President Nixon assured Chiang Kai-shek that America still considered the Republic of China the legal government of the mainland. Japan, also taken by surprise, quickly established diplomatic and trade relations with the People's Republic. Suddenly, China had re-emerged into the world community.

Over the next few years many Americans—students, journalists, and delegates from various organizations—visited China. Their visits were carefully orchestrated to impress them, and, through them, the world. China under the influence of Mao's wife became a vast theater piece for foreign eyes, starring happy peasants and workers, model communes, and thriving socialist industry. With few dissenting voices, the foreigners went home proclaiming that the New China had arrived. The Chinese people knew better, but said nothing; it was illegal even to talk with a foreigner without permission.

China After Mao

Zhou Enlai died in January 1976, and Deng Xiaoping returned from his exile in the countryside to take charge of the national government. In April a massive, unauthorized demonstration was held in Beijing's Tiananmen Square to honor Zhou's memory and thus, by implication, express popular discontent with the policies of the Cultural Revolution. Jiang Qing moved quickly to break up the rally; she accused Deng Xiaoping of failing to maintain control and had him sent off to the countryside once again. But her power was secure only as long as her husband remained alive.

Mao died on September 9; many Chinese believed that his death had been foretold by the catastrophic Tangshan earthquake a few weeks earlier. (Heaven, it seemed, could still bestow or take away imperial power.) Within a few days, a group of moderates seized power in the Central Committee. Deng Xiaoping emerged as China's new paramount leader, although the colorless Hua Guofeng was appointed as the figurehead Acting Chairman of the Communist Party. Jiang Qing and her three closest associates were arrested, along with many underlings; labeled the Gang of Four, they were blamed for deceiving Chairman Mao and perverting the revolution. Over the next two years the new leadership promoted a massive campaign to "criticize the Gang of Four," as every conceivable thing that was wrong with China was attributed to them. Mao himself, in a glass coffin in a vast memorial hall in Tiananmen Square, was seldom criticized directly; respect for China's greatest revolutionary was still too strong. But it was clear that China's new leadership was determined to reverse most of his policies, beginning with the dismantling of the Cultural Revolution. (Jiang Qing and the other members of the Gang of Four were eventually tried for "crimes against the people" and imprisoned.)

In the spring of 1978 the anti–Gang of Four campaign was winding down. The National People's Congress approved a new constitution, and also proclaimed the policy of the "four modernizations." The search for national wealth and power had begun again, with the beginning of drives for rapid modernization of agriculture, industry, science and technology, and defense. Reversing Mao's policy of self-sufficiency, foreign investment and technical advice were encouraged. Universities reopened, and thousands of students were sent to study abroad. Although it was recognized that the Cultural Revolution had resulted in a few genuine accomplishments (such as an extension of health care to rural areas), the period as a whole began to be labeled "the ten terrible years."

The new policies of 1978 met with tremendous public enthusiasm; Deng Xiaoping was seen as the savior of the nation. Enthusiasm soon led, however, to popular calls for still further progress. As the year ended, large, hand-written posters began to appear on walls in downtown Beijing and other big cities—a revival of a traditional way of giving voice to public opinion. Many of the posters called on the government to redress individual injustices suffered during the Cultural Revolution. Others called for comprehensive political and economic reform; one even quoted from the American Declaration of Independence and the Bill of Rights. For several months the government tolerated and even encouraged the posters of "Democracy Wall," but thereafter began to crack down; the most prominent of those who called for "democracy now" were jailed.

On the first day of 1979, the United States and China formally entered into mutual diplomatic relations, completing the process of reconciliation begun by President Nixon seven years before. Each continued to think of the other as a counterweight to the Soviet Union. A small border war between China and Vietnam (by then a firm ally of Russia) in early 1979 was designed to "teach Vietnam a lesson," but was not very successful. Deng Xiaoping and his associates realized that China needed all the foreign support they could get, particularly from the United States and Japan. New codes of civil and criminal law were written—China's legal system had been a shambles since the Cultural Revolution—and pointed out to potential foreign investors as signs of China's new stability. Tourism emerged as a rapidly growing source of foreign exchange income; millions of people abroad (including many overseas Chinese) were eager to see China for themselves. In part because of their cash value as tourist attractions, many historic buildings that had suffered damage during the Cultural Revolution were repaired and opened to the public.

In the early 1980s China embarked on a series of far-reaching reforms designed to implement the four modernizations. In the country-side communes were dismantled and land was leased by the government to individual farm families, who could sell some of their crops on the open market; this led to a rapid increase in agricultural production. Funds were poured into universities, research institutes, and technological development in an effort to create a secure base for further progress. Industrial reform proceeded more slowly, in part because of difficulties in creating new managerial structures to supplement or replace centralized planning, but in some areas—for example, consumer electronics and computers—significant progress was made. A number of Special Economic Zones were created in port cities to encourage foreign investment in export-oriented factories. This was especially effective in attracting investment funds from Hong Kong in the area around Guangzhou.

In order to free national capital for other reforms, China's military budget was cut by nearly 30 percent in the 1980s. To pave the way for military modernization, the size of the army was reduced by one million men. Some of the money thus saved was used to equip the remaining troops with more modern weapons. China's army emerged smaller but much more effective.

The road to reform and modernization has not been entirely smooth. Conservatives in the party and government worry that modernization will lead to the spread of Western liberalism among the Chinese people, and particularly among intellectuals; several (relatively restrained) campaigns have been mounted against "spiritual pollution." Just as Qing Dynasty officials dragged their feet in implementing the self-strengthening reforms of the nineteenth century, some party bureaucrats today have been slow to implement policies that threaten their own privileged status by giving more independent decision-making authority to individual farmers and factory managers. Decentralization of authority has led, in

China's rapid economic modernization has been impressive in many respects, but has also created new problems, such as the severe air pollution seen in this photograph of the industrial city of Lanzhou.

some cases, to corruption and abuses of power. In some areas, particularly environmental protection, meaningful reform has barely begun.
——In 1987, as a symbol of the party's loosening of control over the economy and of the rise of a new generation of Chinese leaders, Deng Xiaoping retired from his various official duties and forced the rest of the "old guard" of Long March veterans to do likewise. (Deng, of course, still retains vast power and prestige behind the scenes.) At the same time, the office of party chairman was abolished; the party is now led by the general secretary, with somewhat reduced authority. China's leadership is now in the hands of a new generation, quiet managers and technocrats in place of the revolutionary heroes of Mao's time. It remains to be seen whether this new leadership will have the nerve to move on to the next logical step in China's reform movement—allowing market prices to

replace, gradually, the centrally planned and entirely artificial price structure that still characterizes China's national economy.

China's emergence as a modernizing, politically stable nation has given it new confidence in foreign affairs. China has signaled its determination to pursue an independent foreign policy, denouncing both America and Russia for "superpower politics" and trying to establish a leading role among the nations of the Third World. Sino-American relations were generally friendly and stable in the 1980s, but China has no interest in becoming a formal American ally. In part to offset any such idea, China has improved relations with the Soviet Union as well, while continuing to insist that full restoration of normal relations will have to wait until Russia reduces its troop strength on the Sino-Soviet frontier, withdraws its troops from Afghanistan, and orders Vietnam to withdraw its troops from Cambodia. Relations with Japan have also been good, although many Chinese remember bitterly Japan's aggression in China during World War II, and worry that new "economic imperialism" will accompany Japanese investment today. China and India remain unfriendly rivals; China's relations with the rest of Asia have improved. Even Taiwan and South Korea, despite their political hostility to the People's Republic, engage in a substantial amount of trade with and investment in China, through intermediaries in Hong Kong. China's principal foreign policy goal today is to show the world that China is stable and unthreatening, so as to attract the foreign investment that is needed to assure continued economic development.

China still is far from having a fully developed economy. Most of what is produced in China is consumed there also; growth in foreign trade has been disappointing. China exports textiles, raw materials, and medium-grade industrial and consumer goods; the foreign exchange thus earned is used, as much as possible, to import manufacturing equipment and high-technology goods. China's goal of self-sufficiency

The Chinese Economy

Grain Production:

Rice:	189,062,000 tons (171,562,000 metric tons) (1985)
Wheat:	94,031,000 tons (85,327,000 metric tons) (1985)
Corn:	68,633,000 tons (62,280,000 metric tons) (1985)

Heavy Industry:

Coal:	991,000,000 tons (899,274,000 metric tons) (1987)
Cement:	198,000,000 tons (179,673,000 metric tons) (1987)
Steel:	62,000,000 tons (56,261,000 metric tons) (1987)
Machine Tools:	146,000 units (1987)

Light Industry:

Bicycles:	40,900,000 units (1987)
TV Sets:	19,400,000 black-and-white units (1987)
	6,700,000 color units (1987)

Textiles:

Silk Fiber:	56,000 tons (50,800 metric tons) (1987)
Silk Fabric:	5.02 billion feet (1.506 billion meters) (1987)
Other Fabric:	55.683 billion feet (16.705 billion meters) (1987)

Foreign Trade (1987)

	TOTAL VALUE OF 2-WAY TRADE	SHARE OF TOTAL FOREIGN TRADE
Hong Kong:	$26.34 billion	31.8%
Japan:	$15.82 billion	19.1%
United States:	$10.41 billion	12.6%

in food and consumer products is designed, in part, to avoid having to use foreign exchange to pay to import those things. Tapping China's huge pool of inexpensive labor to create an export-driven economic boom will continue to require far more economic investment and industrial growth; that still seems to lie well in the future.

Taiwan and Hong Kong

Chiang Kai-shek died in 1975, embittered by America's "betrayal" of the Nationalist cause. He was succeeded as president of the Republic of China by his son, Chiang Ching-kuo. The younger Chiang suffered the further setback of seeing American diplomatic recognition transferred from the Republic to the People's Republic in 1979. Taiwan was left even more diplomatically isolated in the world than the mainland had been ten years before.

Nationalist leaders and Taiwanese businessmen had long since learned, however, to thrive in spite of adversity. American recognition of the People's Republic turned out to be not as bad as it seemed. At the same time, Congress passed the Taiwan Relations Act, which provided for continued American arms sales to Taiwan, and to the establishment of "unofficial" relations between the two countries through offices that were embassies in all but name. Under Chiang Ching-kuo, political relations between Taiwan and the United States improved, if anything, while economic relations boomed. Taiwan's economy grew so robust, in fact, that by the mid 1980s the relationship developed strains of an unexpected kind: Taiwan began to have a huge annual surplus in its trade with the United States, provoking American complaints of unfair trade. Taiwan has emerged as one of Asia's strongest economic powers, with trade and investment links throughout the non-Communist world.

In 1987 President Chiang, old and ill, realized that it was time for political liberalization to accompany Taiwan's economic miracle, and that, for stability's sake, it would have to be done before he died. In a series of bold moves, he ended martial law and legalized opposition political parties, paving the way for the eventual development of genuine democracy in Taiwan. He died early in 1988, and was succeeded by Vice-President Lee Teng-hui, who was born and raised in Taiwan. A Taiwanese president of the Republic of China is a potent symbol of the rise of a new generation in Taiwan, and of the beginning of a new era of popular political participation. President Lee, of course, continues to uphold the view that the Republic is the legal government of China; one of his most difficult long-term problems will be to resist tendencies of many people in Taiwan to simply forget about the mainland and declare that Taiwan should be an independent state. Meanwhile, his government presents itself as the model of success that China itself should follow, both economically and politically; it remains uninterested in contact with the mainland except on its own terms.

Hong Kong, a thriving enclave of capitalism on the South China coast, does not have the option of remaining separate from China. Although Hong Kong itself is British crown land under the 1842 Treaty of Nanjing, much of the present territory of the colony is held on a 99-year lease from China, under an agreement of 1898. In the early 1980s, with the expiration of that lease drawing nearer, Hong Kong's economy developed a severe crisis of confidence: How could long-term investments be made in territory that might be reclaimed by China? After prolonged and difficult negotiations, China and Great Britain agreed in 1983 that all of Hong Kong should revert to Chinese sovereignty in 1997, but that, in return for the British pull-out, China would guarantee that Hong Kong's political, economic, and social systems would remain unchanged for another fifty years. Hong Kong would be

Chinese, but would also be a Special Administrative Region under a formula that the Chinese described as "one country, two systems."

In the mid 1980s Hong Kong's economy recovered rapidly. The dismantling of British colonial rule began in a variety of small ways, and for the first time ever, Hong Kong's citizens acquired a voice in their own government. With the reversion of sovereignty less than a decade away in 1988, Great Britain and China struggled to agree on a Basic Law (constitution) for Hong Kong that would govern the territory's fortunes for another fifty years.

Following the 1983 agreement, China immediately offered to extend the "one country, two systems" formula to Taiwan as well. The Republic of China replied that there was nothing to talk about. With the passage of time, however, indirect trade and investment between China and Taiwan continues to grow, and Taiwanese businessmen have begun routinely (though illegally, from Taiwan's point of view) to travel to China via Hong Kong. In 1988 the Nationalist government relaxed its "no contact" laws slightly to allow people in Taiwan to travel to the mainland to visit relatives. Very slowly, and by very small steps, China's civil war may be fading into history, leaving both sides to wonder what might come next.

Hong Kong, a British Crown Colony since 1842, will return to Chinese sovereignty in 1997. The dynamic growth and spectacular wealth of this enclave of capitalism on the South China coast have served as an example of modernization for China itself.

Daily Life

The Home

Home for four of every five people in China today is likely to be a house in a farm village or small town. It might be a snug cave house in the loess hills of the northwest, or a small adobe dwelling on the North China Plain, but most commonly, rural houses are made of brick. In the most prosperous agricultural regions, the house is also likely to be new; a sharp rise in rural income because of recent economic reforms has led to a tremendous building boom in the countryside. A typical new house is luxurious compared with what it replaced; it might have two stories, with perhaps six rooms and a balcony. The interior is rather plain, with cement floors and plain whitewashed walls. The kitchen, at the back of the house, has a brick stove fueled by coal or wood; the bathroom is a privy in the backyard. There is no central heating, but in North China most houses have a raised brick platform in the main room, through which the heat of the kitchen stove is drawn via ducts before it goes up a chimney. The platform, called a *kang*, retains heat nicely; covered with mats and quilts, it is the center of home life during the cold winter months. The house is surrounded by a dirt farmyard enclosed by a wall. In the back of the house will be a pigpen and a chicken coop.

City dwellers have until recently lived mainly in old-style houses of one or two stories, jammed closely together with their plain walled fronts facing onto streets or alleys. In recent years these deteriorating houses have increasingly been replaced by apartment buildings of six or eight stories. These new buildings are plain and crowded, but they are sturdy, clean, and equipped with running water. They are less picturesque that the old houses they replace, but from the point of view of the people who live in them, they are more comfortable and convenient. A typical apartment in a new building is small, usually two or three rooms; in many cases, two apartments share a single kitchen and bathroom. Apartments are plainly furnished with inexpensive new items and, perhaps, a family heirloom bed or table. Recently acquired modern appliances—a sewing machine, record player, television—are proudly on display.

Whether in the country or the city, three generations usually live under one roof. In most cases, a family consists of grandparents, a grown son, and his wife and children. Although this leads to crowded quarters, the old people play an important role in the family. Because both husband and wife are likely to have full-time jobs, whether in the fields or in some urban employment, the grandmother, especially, baby-sits and helps with the housework. If the grandfather is in his sixties or older, he will enjoy the privileges of age by spending much of his time with his friends, enjoying his retirement and doing little work. Nominally the head of the family, in practice he often will defer to his

working son. In part to help ensure that there will be enough jobs for younger people, the government encourages people to retire early—usually by age fifty-five in the case of urban workers, although in the countryside older people often continue to work on farms for as long as they are able to.

A Chinese married woman will rely on her mother-in-law to help with child care and light housework, but the main burden of keeping house still falls upon her. After finishing her day's work on the job, she must take primary responsibility for marketing (with no refrigerators, this must be done every day), cooking, cleaning, and laundry. Very recently, small washing machines have begun to make life easier for millions of women in China. Except for home repairs and some child care, men seldom share very much in the burdens of household work.

In cities, towns, and villages alike, neighborhood associations play an important role in everyone's life. Based on the ancient Chinese idea of mutual responsibility, the neighborhood associations rely especially on retired people to serve as the eyes and ears of the community. "The grannies," as everyone calls them, take note of any strangers in the neighborhood, and watch out for fires or crime. They also feel free to scold any younger person who departs from community standards in appearance or behavior. A man who drinks too much, a woman who beats her children, a young man who likes long hair and flashy clothes—all can expect a visit from members of the neighborhood association, telling them to change their ways. Today as in the past, social control in China depends more on community pressure than on the force of law.

Cave house built into a loess cliff, Shaanxi Province. Houses like this one—dry, comfortable, and roomy—have been built in the loess hills of northwestern China since ancient times.

Work

Farmwork   Most Chinese are farmers, but the nature of rural work has changed dramatically in recent years. Between the mid 1950s and the early 1980s, farmlands were owned collectively by communes. State planning authorities told the communes what crops to raise and how much they were expected to produce. At the end of the year, all commune members shared in the commune's profits on the basis of the "work points" they had accumulated. Since the early 1980s, that plan has been replaced by the "responsibility system," in which individual farm families hold long-term leases on land that they farm alone. Grain, cotton, and oilseeds are still grown according to quotas; each family raises its share and sells it to the state for a fixed price. Having fulfilled that responsibility, the family can choose to grow anything it wants, and sell it at a free-market price. Especially in agricultural areas near large urban markets, this has led to large increases in farm income. Many farm families now choose to specialize in particular market crops, such as fresh vegetables, pork, ducks, fish raised in artificial ponds, or even cut flowers.

Communes employed more people than were needed for efficient production. The responsibility system has produced a surplus of labor in the countryside, because efficient production is now economically rewarded. The labor surplus has created both problems and opportunities. The problem is the threat of rural unemployment and the desire of the unemployed to move to the cities. In order to prevent further urban crowding, internal migration is firmly controlled. In all large cities, residence permits are required; without one, it is not possible legally to find a place to live, a job, or to obtain grain, oil, and clothing ration coupons. Unable to migrate to the cities, surplus rural labor must take advantage of, or even create, local opportunities, and this too has led to an increase in rural prosperity. Some rural families have given up farming altogether, except for their own gardens, and now specialize in transporting crops to market for other people, in brick making and construction (for all those new houses), or in running small businesses, such as repair shops. In other cases, one or two members of a family will work full-time or part-time in a local factory. With government encouragement, much of China's recent industrial growth has been in the form of small, rural factories producing a wide variety of labor-intensive products.

For those who remain full-time farmers, life follows a familiar cycle of plowing, planting, tending, and harvesting. But there have been changes in farm work as well. Fertilizers, pesticides, and herbicides (all often used too heavily, with damaging environmental results) have made work easier and productivity greater, as have new, high-yield hybrid seeds. "Iron oxen"—small, two-wheeled walking tractors with simple, easily maintained engines—have replaced muscle-power in many tasks, both in the fields and for haulage. For all that, farming remains, as it has always been, very hard work.

Industrial Work
With the exception of small, family-run businesses, almost all industrial and commercial enterprises in China are owned by the state. Many factories and large stores are owned by city, town, or county governments; very large factories, mines, oilfields, railroads, and so on are owned by the national government. Most industrial and commercial workers, therefore, are employed by the state, through their work units. In return for low wages, little choice in job assignments, and often unsatisfactory working conditions, workers are protected by the "iron ricebowl"—guaranteed lifetime employment. This has led to overemployment and severe inefficiency in China's urban economy. Efforts are now being made to extend the responsibility

system to the industrial and commercial sectors, with managers being given more authority over products, profits, and the utilization of labor; efficient operations are rewarded with bonuses and higher levels of investment in new plants and equipment. In order to reduce overstaffing of factories and provide a better level of services to people in cities, the government has encouraged urban workers to set up small-scale private enterprises, such as restaurants, repair shops, tailoring and dress-making shops, and beauty parlors. Progress has been made in all of these areas, but work for many people in China's cities still means long hours in overcrowded, poorly lit factories using equipment that is often obsolete and sometimes unsafe, producing goods that are old-fashioned in design. Workers in large stores, restaurants, and other service industries complain about being overburdened and underpaid, while customers complain about poor service and inadequate products. Modernization remains more a goal than a reality for China's industrial sector; meanwhile, many urban workers envy the new-found comparative wealth of their country cousins.

White-Collar Work

The country that invented bureaucratic government continues to employ tens of millions of people in government offices. White-collar work is generally regarded as more desirable and prestigious than industrial work, in part because it is easier and cleaner, and in part because of old social attitudes about the importance of literacy—and working with words—as a mark of status. Virtually all office workers are, directly or indirectly, government employees; the same problems of overstaffing and inefficiency that cause difficulties in industry and commerce are found in bureaucracies of all kinds. In part this is because of the nature of the Chinese written language. Chinese typewriters are slow and clumsy, and require a high degree of skill; many documents are copied out by hand and duplicated by mimeograph

A ball-bearing factory, Luoyang. One goal of the four modernizations is to upgrade China's industrial equipment, which now is often obsolete and unsafe.

or other printing processes. (The availability of microcomputers with software and printers capable of generating and printing Chinese characters quickly and easily is about to revolutionize office life in China.) In part, however, the bureaucracy has been used to absorb a large number of well-educated workers, providing employment rather than work; the result is waste and duplication of effort. In the spring of 1988, the Chinese government announced plans to cut the number of office workers by 20 percent over the next few years. The proposal has been greeted by skepticism, however, and it is not clear how the surplus workers would be absorbed by other sectors of the economy.

Intellectuals, such as teachers, professors, doctors, research workers, and high-level officials, continue to enjoy some of the high status that they have always had in Chinese society, although they are paid only slightly more than industrial or bureaucratic workers. In virtually all cases, these workers too are employees of the state.

Fewer than five percent of China's people are members of the Chinese Communist Party; Party membership is a privilege, not a right. At all levels of society, Party membership is a source of prestige and influence. The Party employs large numbers of people directly. These cadres, as they are called, are assigned to offices, factories, army units, and local governments to ensure that the plans of the ruling Party are carried out, to encourage support for the government, to perform political education, and to serve as intermediaries between ordinary people and the state. Party workers, accustomed to acting as agents of political control, are to some extent threatened by the increased individual and organizational initiative that lies at the heart of the present "responsibility system" economic reforms.

The *danwei*, or work unit, is a crucial factor in the life of every Chinese worker. Workers deal with the state through their work units, which arrange residence permits in cities and land leases in the countryside, as well as ration coupons, access to schools and hospitals, and passports for travel or study abroad. Large enterprises often offer a wide range of social services to their workers, including day-care services, schools, clinics, and recreational facilities. In China, groups rather than individuals have always formed the basis of society; the *danwei* is the economic equivalent of an extended family.

Although economic reform has produced rural prosperity and the prospect of bonuses for urban workers in efficient enterprises, Chinese workers still earn very little money. The average industrial wage is under $50 per month. However, the cost of living is also very low.

Urban apartments, subsidized by city governments or large work units, rent for a few dollars a month. Grain, cooking oil, meat, and cotton cloth are rationed, but are also heavily subsidized to reduce their retail prices. The growth of a free-market economy has led to a greater availability of fresh food and attractive clothing, but at somewhat higher prices. Elementary education is free, and higher-level education and medical care cost almost nothing. Almost everyone can afford the essentials of life, but consumer goods and luxuries remain expensive. Most families must save for several months, for example, to afford a bicycle or a color television.

Education

Six years of elementary education are compulsory in China, and the government has made basic education widely available except in the most remote and backward parts of the country. Many children, especially in the countryside, leave school after six years. In rural areas, middle schools and high schools tend to be located in towns rather than in villages, making them less accessible; moreover, in the countryside, with the responsibility system, extra available labor, even from children, can translate directly into higher family income. In the cities, most children complete middle school, and a smaller percentage go on to high school. University education, though highly prized, is available only to a few. The number of freshman-class places available every year is far smaller than the number of applicants, and the university entrance examinations are very difficult. In an effort to compensate for the lack of higher education, many large work units have technical schools and other educational programs for their workers. In premodern China, only a fortunate few could read and write; today, about 80 percent of China's people are literate at a basic level.

Chinese schools are plain and simple, with books and equipment limited to the bare essentials. Special advanced schools for brilliant children might have well-stocked libraries and well-equipped laboratories; most schools do not. Educational methods tend to be traditional and conservative. Students listen and take notes as their teachers lecture; memorization and rote recitation are encouraged; open discussion in the classroom is rare.

Because both fathers and mothers usually have full-time jobs, many Chinese children begin nursery school at around the age of two. Young children in China, both at home and in school, are treated with great kindness and indulgence. Dressed in brightly colored clothing, nursery school children receive a great deal of attention from their teachers. Small children are virtually never spanked; discipline consists of attempting, first, to distract a naughty child with some other activity. If that fails, the child is made to sit alone for a while, deprived of the company of his or her playmates. Even at this very early age, social values are at the heart of education. Children are encouraged to share toys, to cooperate, and to avoid arguing or fighting. Group activities, such as singing and organized games, are stressed; solitary play is discouraged. Painting and drawing prepare young hands for the task of learning to write.

By the first grade, children have begun the long task of learning to read and write several thousand Chinese characters. The curriculum also includes mathematics and lessons in history that emphasize the accomplishments of the Chinese revolution and the Chinese Communist Party. From the earliest grades onward, education follows a standard national curriculum aimed at the mastery of a certain body of knowledge rather than at encouraging independent thinking. From middle school onward, the curriculum includes foreign languages. English and Japanese are the most widely studied; there, too, reading and recitation are

Children in a kindergarten in Luoyang. The main goal of education for very young children is to teach the value of cooperation within a group setting.

emphasized, conversational skills are not. At the university level, regardless of subject matter, required courses predominate over elective ones.

Since the early 1980s, thousands of Chinese students have studied abroad in the United States, Japan, Western Europe, Eastern Europe, and Russia. Most of the students who study abroad have already completed a university degree and have been sent to acquire specialized postgraduate education. Many of these students abroad are bewildered at first by the greater expectations of individual initiative, and lower level of supervision, that they encounter. When they return home after several years, having gotten used to a less structured life abroad, they often find it difficult to fit again into the relatively inflexible organization of their work unit. Within Communist Party circles there has been a continuing debate about how to take advantage of the skills these students learn abroad, while avoiding social disruption caused by any "foreign" or "bourgeois" attitudes they may have picked up along the way.

When students in rural areas leave school, they typically work on their own families' farms. Those who do not, and also most students in nonrural areas, are assigned jobs in factories or offices by the state labor bureau, in consultation with the students' teachers. Some, hoping for better work assignments later on, will volunteer for duty in the armed forces, though not all volunteers are accepted. Like other large organizations in China, the armed forces offer further educational opportunities for their members. Job assignments are usually permanent. As in the old days, upward mobility in China today comes primarily through education. Once out of school, opportunities for advancement, except up the slow ladder of seniority within a single organization, are rare.

Love, Marriage, and Children

China today is, as it always has been, a socially conservative country. Casual relations between the sexes are deeply disapproved of. Even among teenagers, most activities are group activities, and dating is uncommon. Love is romanticized as an idea, but most young people have been raised to be too shy to do much about it. Personal privacy is rare; a boy and a girl seen in each other's company more than a few times will be the subjects of gossip. Young people are discouraged from thinking about serious relationships until they are in their twenties.

Not surprisingly, therefore, most marriages in China result from introductions arranged by parents, relatives, or other third parties. Old-style arranged marriages, in which the two people involved were strangers on their wedding day, are a thing of the past, but most young people rely on others to help them find a suitable mate. Managers of work units, for example, will often introduce a young man and a young woman who have each expressed an interest in finding someone to marry.

When young men are asked what they are looking for in a wife, they are likely to specify that she should be attractive, good-tempered and somewhat submissive, and that she have a good job. Women want men of good moral character who are kind, reasonably well educated, and employed in good jobs. Very well educated young women sometimes have difficulty in marrying; they want a husband at least as well educated as they are, while many men are suspicious of intellectual women. In recent years women have increasingly insisted that their future husbands have a significant amount of money saved up, and be ready to begin married life by setting up a house complete with bicycle, television, sewing machine, record player, and washing machine. Marriages that result from introductions are likely to put greater weight on such criteria as suitability and economic resources; modern love-matches (still relatively rare) tend to rely on emotional bonds to overcome other difficulties.

Marriages often are delayed while the two people involved, and their families, negotiate the details of the match. Further delays may result as the couple waits for the propective husband's work unit to assign them an apartment. Finally, however, the wedding day arrives. The actual marriage ceremony consists of signing a marriage register in a local government office. In rural areas, this is often now supplemented with a religious ceremony at a Buddhist or Daoist temple. The real celebration, however, comes at a wedding banquet, paid for by the parents of both partners. Despite government disapproval, these banquets nowadays are often lavish and expensive. In large cities, it has also become fashionable to record the marriage with formal photographs, with the couple wearing a rented western-style formal suit and wedding dress.

The One-Child Family

In an effort to control the growth of China's population, the Chinese government has set up a system of rewards and penalties designed to encourage one-child families. Couples are urged to sign pledges that they will have only one child and receive a bonus for doing so. If they subsequently have two or more children, however, they must pay a heavy fine, and also pay for the education and medical care for the "extra" children. In rural areas, exceptions are often made to allow families to have two children, especially if the first one is a girl or is physically handicapped; members of ethnic minorities are partly or totally exempt from family-planning rules.

In general this system has worked fairly well, and China's population growth has slowed dramatically since the mid 1970s. In recent years rural prosperity has led to somewhat greater population growth in the countryside again, but overall China's "population bomb" is no longer ticking quite so loudly. At the same time, the policy has led to a number of problems. First, government agencies, and neighborhood associations and work units acting on behalf of the government, sometimes put severe psychological pressure on women to have abortions rather than give birth to second children. This has produced both personal unhappiness and a sense of social unease; it has also been severely criticized abroad. Second, although the typical Chinese preference for sons over daughters is less strong than it was in the old days, it still exists. As

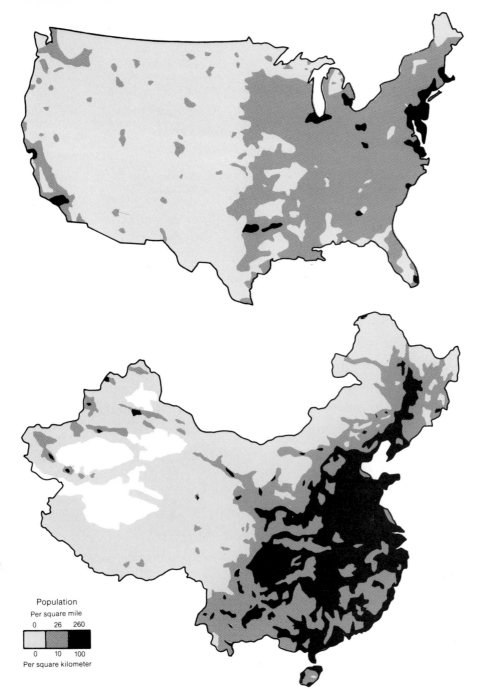

Population

Per square mile

| 0 | 26 | 260 |

| 0 | 10 | 100 |

Per square kilometer

Population Maps: U.S. and China, Population Density Compared

a popular saying puts it, "The birth of a son is a big happiness; the birth of a daughter is a small happiness." Some couples have used medical tests to determine the sex of a fetus and have used abortion if the fetus is a girl so as to try again for a boy. In extreme cases, infant girls have been murdered (usually in rural areas, and usually by the husband's parents) in the hope that the next child, still within the one-child-family limit, will be a boy. These practices are illegal; infanticide is murder, and is punished as such. But both infanticide and sex-selective abortion do sometimes occur.

Another, though less severe, problem of the one-child family is what has become known as the "little emperor syndrome." Children in one-child families are often indulged to a degree that is extreme even by child-loving Chinese standards. Some older people wonder whether such "spoiled" children will ever grow up to be responsible, self-disciplined adults. Older people also wonder who, in a world of few children, will care for and shelter the elderly, as tradition has always demanded of the young.

Divorce

Legal procedures for divorce are relatively easy in China, but divorce itself is uncommon. Most people enter into marriage with expectations of stability, security, and affection, but not necessarily romance; society as a whole expects married couples to be accommodating and work to keep a marriage together. If a couple does file for divorce, the family-court judge is likely to order them to work toward a reconciliation, with the aid of the neighborhood association and their work units. Only when all efforts fail is a divorce granted; at that point property is divided, child custody is established, and both parties often return to live with their parents again. Divorced people are viewed with some disapproval and regarded as unreliable marriage partners, and so often find difficulty in marrying again. This, too, often leads people to make the best of an uncomfortable situation, rather than face the prospect of remaining unmarried after a divorce.

The Rhythm of Daily Life

Like farmers everywhere, Chinese farmers adjust their work schedules to meet the needs of their crops. Work is heavy during some parts of the growing cycle, and light during others. Many people in the countryside now engage in sideline activities, such as making traditional handicrafts, to produce extra cash during slack periods. The daily lives of workers in factories and offices are more regulated by routine. Most

A poultry market in southeastern China. The creation of a free-market system for many agricultural goods in 1979 has led to a significant expansion of production. Note the bicycles, used to transport goods as well as people.

people work six days per week; the school week also runs from Monday through Saturday. In the largest cities, many workers have staggered work schedules, so that not everyone has a day off on the same day of the week.

For most people the day begins early. Breakfast consists of rice porridge, with small side dishes of pickled vegetables, dried fish, or boiled eggs, and tea. Street vendors make the rounds of neighborhoods, selling sesame biscuits, fried crullers, and hot soybean milk as extra breakfast treats. After breakfast the rush hour begins, as millions of urban workers and students in crowded buses or on bicycles go off to work or to school. Many people carry box lunches with them, or eat at cafeterias at the workplace or school. Lunch is a simple meal, based on rice, noodles, or bread (steamed, not baked), again with small side dishes. After a final glass of tea, everyone relaxes during the after-lunch rest hour before taking up tasks again. In the late afternoon, urban streets again become rivers of buses and bicycles carrying people home at the end of the day. On the way, people might stop at a vendor's stand for snacks of steamed buns, fried dumplings, or fruit.

As soon as she arrives home, a working mother begins to prepare supper. Again, the meal is based on rice, noodles, or steamed bread, but the side dishes are larger in the evening: They might consist of stir-fried vegetables, soybean cakes, or, more rarely, eggs, fish, or meat. The meal begins and ends with tea, but the food itself is accompanied by boiled water or beer. Ordinary meals do not include dessert; the last course is usually soup.

Father and son, Chengdu. Most Chinese rely on bicycles for personal transportation. Old-style urban houses, like those in the background, are now rapidly being replaced by high-rise apartment houses.

Leisure

Evenings are usually spent at home. Television and radio provide the main sources of entertainment for the evening hours. They also carry educational programs, and tens of millions of people in China follow the nightly television lessons in learning English. Movies, traditional operas, theater, variety shows, circuses and acrobatic shows, and other entertainments are regularly available in cities, less often in towns and villages; but for most people, a night out is a treat rather than a regular event. By ten o'clock, most people are in bed.

In a recent public-opinion poll in Beijing, a majority of the people surveyed expressed dissatisfaction with the amount and quality of leisure activities available to them. In other cities the situation is the same, and in small towns and villages it is worse. The two most common activities for urban workers on their days off are shopping (or window shopping) and visiting parks. Most of China's parks were once the private gardens of the upper class; many people today feel a strong sense of satisfaction in being able to stroll through the emperor's Forbidden City or Summer Palace. In very recent years, the crowds at the most popular sight-seeing places, such as the Great Wall or the Ming tombs, have included not only local residents but also groups of Chinese vacationers on tours organized by their work units.

Sports are also popular leisure activities. The most common are those that require little space and equipment, such as table tennis, badminton, and basketball. Sports that involve expensive equipment and facilities—skiing, tennis, and sailing, for example—are quite unusual. The most common form of exercise is the traditional breath-control and fitness routine called *taijiquan*, which requires no equipment at all. Spectator sports are also popular; large urban stadiums attract tens of thousands of people to watch soccer and basketball matches.

Food provides the focus for China's favorite recreational activity, the

Taiwan's New Middle Class

A generation or two ago, daily life in Taiwan was fairly similar to that in the People's Republic of China today. Most people lived in villages or small towns and depended on agriculture for their livelihoods. Leisure activities and consumer spending were restricted by modest incomes and scarce resources. Today, that situation has been drastically altered by Taiwan's sustained economic boom. Most people in Taiwan now live in cities and work in manufacturing, service industries, or white-collar occupations. Half the population is under the age of twenty-five. A sharp rise in disposable income has fueled an enthusiastic consumer society; the average apartment in Taiwan is crammed with electric and electronic appliances of all kinds. Leisure activities continue far into the night—Taipei's cinemas all have midnight shows, and there are dozens of all-night videotape parlors. Vacation trips, high-fashion clothing, motorcycles, and expensive restaurant meals are all easily within the means of Taiwan's new middle class. The rise of the middle class has also produced a generation gap, as frugal parents worry about the free-spending habits of their children. A lively debate is now being carried on in Taiwan's newspapers and magazines: Are middle-class values expressed in money alone? Will a flowering of contemporary culture follow in the wake of Taiwan's material prosperity, or will Taiwan become just another Hong Kong, worshipping at the altar of the god of wealth?

banquet party. A banquet is likely to accompany any special occasion: a wedding, the birth of a child, the building of a new farmhouse or the negotiation of a business contract, the arrival of visiting friends or relatives, or the annual New Year holiday. Unlike grain-based ordinary meals, banquets emphasize elaborately prepared courses of, for example, pork or chicken stir fried with vegetables, roast duck, fried whole fish, and specialties like shellfish or sea cucumbers. Beer, wine, and potent sorghum brandy accompany the food; custom demands that a toast be proposed whenever wine or brandy is drunk. Complaints in official government newspapers about the frequency and cost of banquets nowadays tend to fall on deaf ears among people for whom food is truly one of the finer things of life.

Coping

Life in China is crowded, often routine, and frequently hemmed in by countless rules and regulations. In China, as everywhere else, the quality of life depends not only on enjoying pleasures but on ways of coping with the humdrum. People have become adept at creating psychological personal space in the midst of crowds. Because swollen bureaucracies at every level of government have made even such things as buying a bicycle or a long-distance train ticket a nightmare of filling out forms, people have learned to circumvent regulations by, as they say, "going through the back door." People trade favors through networks of family and friends to obtain scarce goods and services and cut through red tape. This sometimes crosses the line into outright corruption and influence peddling, but for most people most of the time, the need to bend the rules a little is a simple fact of life.

Daily life for most people in China seldom rises above the level of the ordinary. But almost everyone is economically secure, well fed, well clothed, and adequately housed. Within a very few years, the Chinese government is likely to feel a rising public demand for more consumer goods and more and better leisure time. For now, in a country where famine, disease, and homelessness are still living memories, an ordinary life strikes most people as being very good indeed.

The Future of China

Every Chinese person alive today, whether in China or anywhere else in the world, is an heir to one of the oldest and greatest civilizations ever developed. Although modern revolutionary movements in China have sometimes tried quite violently to repudiate the past in order to make way for the future, China has remained uniquely itself. The Chinese language, a shared sense of what constitutes civilized behavior, the importance of the family as the basic unit of society, and pride in the glories of China's past all contribute to what it means to be Chinese. The continued strength of Chinese culture and national identity has enabled China to survive the grim problems of the past century and a half of its history. It will continue to provide a foundation as China moves into a future that is both uncertain and hopeful.

From the May Fourth Movement to the Cultural Revolution, many patriotic Chinese have felt that it is necessary for China to discard the burden of the past in order to create a strong, modern nation. It is certainly true that some aspects of China's historical legacy are reactionary and harmful. The civilization that invented a bureaucratic government staffed by a professional civil service now too often finds itself mired in mindless bureaucratism, as petty officials guard their privileges and pay more attention to minute regulations than to efficiency, equity, and common sense. The old Chinese ruling class theoretically won its position in society on the basis of merit, but often took its elite status of wealth and power for granted, regarding more ordinary people with condescension or contempt. Elitism lives on in China, despite socialist attempts to create a classless society. The ethnic Han habit of treating non-Han peoples within the Middle Kingdom as "barbarians" also lingers on, hampering attempts to turn the People's Republic of China into a genuinely multiethnic, multicultural nation.

As recent history has shown, all efforts to discard China's past seem doomed by the sheer strength of China's historical and cultural legacy. Even if they were not, a China cut off from its past would be adrift in a modern world where national identity and self-confidence provide moorings in a sea of change. Turning its back on its past, China would have to reinvent a national identity in the present; could the result be, in the foreseeable future, anything but a feeble and humiliating imitation of the West?

As China's national leadership now clearly proclaims, the challenge of the future for China is to remain Chinese but also to become modern. Both continuity and change are essential. Whether the task of creating this hoped-for modern China can be accomplished in the near future will depend on how several major challenges are met.

The first challenge is to create a presence for China in the world that is appropriate for a large nation, rich in resources, inhabited by one fifth of humanity. The search for "wealth and power" that has motivated Chinese nationalists for over one hundred years must go on. China is now engaged in a series of economic reforms—the "four modernizations" and the "responsibility system"—whose success is in doubt. It is not yet clear whether the Chinese Communist Party has the courage to pursue the kind of political reform that will make economic reform possible. If the reform movement does continue, and if it does lead to success, it will probably resemble a model that is already in place in the three Chinese states of Asia that are not under the control of the People's Republic of China. In Hong Kong, Singapore, and the Republic of China on Taiwan (and also in South Korea, with its strong Confucian heritage), a considerable degree of economic freedom coexists with much more restricted political freedom. Although there are signs that genuine political democracy is beginning to emerge in all of those states, until very recently the political life of each has been wholly dominated by a single ruling party (or, in the case of Hong Kong, a British colonial government). At the same time, their governments have encouraged a high degree of individual initiative in both the private and the public creation of wealth. The result has been an era of phenomenally rapid economic growth in each of the "Four Tigers" (as Taiwan, Hong Kong, Singapore, and South Korea are now often called), accompanied by a slow but steady expansion of personal and political freedom.

Until very recently, China's economy has been totally dominated by a sluggish and cumbersome central planning authority. A commitment to socialist principles of equality led the government to prefer slow growth for everyone over more rapid but unequal economic advancement. Individual initiative risked being labeled "bourgeois" or even "counterrevolutionary." Party and government officials strengthened their power and privileges by maintaining strict control over the economy. Economic reform threatens some of the most deeply held beliefs of conservative Chinese Communists. Private control of capital and private "exploitation of labor" are both looked upon with deep suspicion. Socialism, in this view, demands that the dominant role of the public economic sector must not be challenged by private initiative. Any policy that might lead to the reemergence of social classes based on unequal distribution of wealth will be seen by conservatives as a step back toward the bad old days of elitism and wealth for the few, suffering and poverty for the many.

Billboards line a promenade along the Pearl River in Guangzhou. The opening of China's markets to foreign products symbolizes, for many Chinese, both the promise of economic modernization and the danger of "spiritual pollution."

Nevertheless, if China's current goal of creating "socialism with Chinese characteristics" is to succeed at all, it is likely to prove much more traditionally Chinese and much less socialist than the national leadership now imagines. Nationalism and cultural identity are the real foundations of modern Chinese ideology. China's greatest hope of attaining a position of international standing based on national wealth and power lies in economic reform. China's leaders might learn from their smaller neighbors that economic liberalization need not challenge the dominant position of the ruling party, nor threaten its goal of establishing a stable, orderly, and just society. In the long run, they may also learn that a certain amount of "bourgeois liberalization" will simply have to be tolerated.

A second factor in China's search for wealth and power in the international arena is the need to establish a reputation for stability and reliability. The political upheavals that shook the People's Republic between 1949 and 1976 have led both ordinary Chinese citizens and the world community to doubt that any policy of the Chinese government can be relied upon to remain stable in the long run. No one knows when a change in the political winds at the highest levels of government might lead to a 180-degree shift in policy. This has led to suspicion of authority and apathy at home, and a lack of confidence abroad. China's current policy of encouraging foreign investment and joint ventures must be trustworthy if it is to succeed.

China's international position also depends on cultivating a reputation as a reliable great power and a safe, friendly neighbor in Asia itself. Both the United States and the Soviet Union have sometimes had exaggerated fears of China as an "expansionist" power; historically China has not sought to extend its control much beyond its present borders. China's imperial ambitions are old and familiar: control of Tibet and the Silk Route corridor in Central Asia, and establishment of a sphere of influence over the smaller nations on its borders. Nevertheless, China's present international reputation will depend in part on treating Tibet and other ethnic minority territories as genuine autonomous regions within a multiethnic state, rather than as colonies; on living up to its promise of self-government for Hong Kong after 1997; and on refraining from meddling in the affairs of its small neighbors. Doing so will ensure China's ability to have secure relations with the United States, the Soviet Union, Japan, and Western Europe, and to attract investment and trade from the wealthy small nations of East Asia. Ultimately it would also enhance the possibility of a reconciliation with Taiwan.

Another crucial challenge for China is the need to stabilize the size of its population. The population explosion that began in the seventeenth century and accelerated in the eighteenth has been the source of many of China's woes in the modern era, quite apart from the impact of the West. The relentless need to find food for an increasing number of mouths, the strain of overpopulation on government services, and the social pressure of extreme population density in some areas have all had to take priority, distracting China's leaders from the many tasks needed to transform the nation into an effective modern state. On an individual level, economic reform works against population control, as families feel they both need and can afford more children to contribute to family income. On the national level, economic reform that leads only to population growth would be a disaster. On the other hand, if the policy of stabilizing the population at its current size does succeed, it will create a new problem for the future. For several decades, the percentage

A group of boys on a school outing, in Hunan Province, proudly displays a new cassette player. Economic reform in China has led to a sharp rise in personal income, and to an increased demand for consumer products.

The Plight of the Panda

The giant panda is instantly recognizable as a symbol of China. The panda is a large, playful, unaggressive animal, distantly related to bears and raccoons; its diet consists almost entirely of bamboo leaves. Its striking black-and-white markings give it a doll-like appearance that almost everyone finds endearing. Sadly, the panda is also seriously in danger of extinction. Only a few hundred survive in the wild, confined mainly to the Wolong Panda Reserve and other protected forests in Sichuan Province. In the early 1980s an international panda-rescue campaign was mounted to save those endangered few from starvation when, in a natural cycle, much of the wild bamboo in their territory died off. A captive breeding program in China has begun to show some success, but not enough to compensate for mortality in the wild.

Despite Chinese panda-protection programs and international aid, it is not clear that wild pandas will be able to survive for many more years. The killing of pandas is strictly prohibited—some panda hunters have been executed—but there are people in the world who are willing to pay thousands of dollars for a panda-skin rug, and poaching continues. Relentless population pressure and environmental mismanagement have led to a drastic shrinking of the panda's natural habitat. Pandas are slow to mature and produce few young, making them poorly resistant to environmental shocks.

The panda thus has become not only a symbol of China, but of China's commitment to environmental management. If the fate of the panda remains in doubt, how much more precarious is the plight of the Yangtse alligator, the red-crowned crane, and hundreds of other endangered species? Their survival will depend on China's ability to pursue modernization wisely.

of elderly people in the population will increase; a society that has traditionally depended on families to support the elderly will find itself faced with a need to provide publicly a broad range of social and medical services for its senior citizens.

Finally, China must continue to redefine its sense of national identity and national culture after the fall of an imperial system that had endured for over two thousand years. Many of the glories of China's past were the products of a ruling class that dominated the nation's wealth, power, prestige, and access to education. That class was swept away by the revolution that accompanied China's emergence into the modern world. Its values and accomplishments now belong largely to the past. China's modern culture must, from now on, emerge from a broad popular base but still satisfy China's historical self-image as a fountainhead of cultural excellence. Hand in hand with pride in the past must go a new pride in China's modern arts, literature, music, and other cultural accomplishments. China's greatness in the long-term future depends both on being modern *and* on remaining Chinese.

China's current situation has been drastically altered by the growth of a student-led movement for democracy and human rights, followed by its brutal suppression. As this book goes to press, a wave of arrests and executions seems to confirm that the hard-liners are in control of the country, but at the cost of a severe setback to reform at home and grave damage to China's reputation abroad.

The photographs on the following pages capture some of the spirit of hope and anguish that marked China in the spring of 1989.

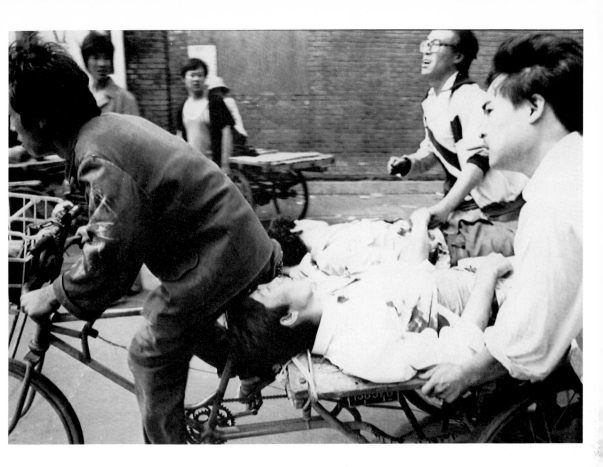

In May, 1989, massive demonstrations of students and workers agitating for democratic reforms occupied center stage in Beijing's Tiananmen Square, overshadowing a summit meeting between Deng Xiaoping and Soviet Party Leader Mikhail Gorbachev. Defying a declaration of martial law, for more than two weeks demonstrators succeeded in preventing troops from entering the city, while many soldiers emotionally declared that they would never open fire on the students. At the end of the month, the students erected a statue of the "Goddess of Freedom and Democracy" in the Square. (left)

On June 4, military forces acting under new orders occupied Beijing and drove the demonstrators from Tiananmen Square, inflicting severe casualties. (above) This action provoked outrage among the Chinese people and around the world, casting doubt on the future stability of the Chinese government. Both photos AP/Wide World Photos.

Bibliography

Thousands of books are available on special subjects in Chinese history, culture, and society. This bibliography lists only reference works, broad topical studies, sources of up-to-date information on contemporary China, and nonprint resources.

Reference Works and Broad Topical Studies

The Cambridge History of China. 14 Vols. Cambridge, England: Cambridge University Press, 1978– .

A comprehensive history of China from the Han Dynasty to the mid-twentieth century.

The Encyclopedia of Asian History. 4 Vols. New York: Charles Scribner's Sons, 1987.

An excellent reference work, covering all of Asia. Prepared under the auspices of The Asia Society.

The Cambridge Encyclopedia of China. Cambridge, England: Cambridge University Press, 1982.

A convenient one-volume history of China, arranged topically.

The Encyclopedia of Religion. 16 Vols. New York: Macmillan, 1986.

> Excellent topical coverage of Chinese religion and philosophy.

Jacques Gernet. *A History of Chinese Civilization.* Cambridge: Cambridge University Press, 1982.

> The best of many comprehensive histories of China.

Joseph Needham. *Science and Civilisation in China.* 7 Vols. in multiple parts. Cambridge: Cambridge University Press, 1956– .

> Encyclopedic coverage of Chinese science and technology in the context of social history.

James Legge. *The Chinese Classics.* 5 Vols. Oxford: Oxford University Press, 1893; various reprint editions.

> Legge's translations of the basic texts of Confucianism are old but still standard.

Yu-lan Fung. *A History of Chinese Philosophy.* Derk Bodde, tr. 2 Vols. Princeton: Princeton University Press, 1952–53.

> Surveys Chinese philosophy from antiquity to the twentieth century; the standard work in the field.

Wm. Theodore de Bary et al. *Sources of Chinese Tradition.* New York: Columbia University Press, 1960.

> Translations of basic documents of Chinese religion, philosophy, and political and social history.

Laurence Sickman and Alexander Soper. *The Art and Architecture of China.* Harmondsworth, England: Penguin Books, 1956.

> The best one-volume survey of Chinese painting, sculpture, and architecture.
>
> Recent archaeological finds have made some portions of this book out of date.

William H. Nienhauser, Jr., ed. *The Indiana Companion to Traditional Chinese Literature.* Bloomington: Indiana University Press, 1986.

> Informative historical and critical essays on all aspects of traditional Chinese literature.

Bibliographies

Charles O. Hucker. *China: A Critical Bibliography.* Tucson: University of Arizona Press, 1962.

> Somewhat out of date but clearly organized and convenient to use. A good place to start.

G. William Skinner, ed. *Modern Chinese Society: An Analytical Bibliography.* Vol. 1,
Publications in Western Languages. Stanford: Stanford University Press, 1973.

Comprehensive coverage of works on China for the period 1644–1972.

Bibliography of Asian Studies. Ann Arbor, MI: Association for Asian Studies, annual.

The best source for recent publications on China and all of Asia.

Contemporary Affairs

China Briefing. Boulder, CO: Westview Press, annual.

An annual update on Chinese affairs, prepared by the China Council of The Asia
Society.

Asian Yearbook. Hong Kong: Far Eastern Economic Review, annual.

Brief country-by-country surveys of the year under review, with emphasis on
political events and economics.

Statistical Yearbook for Asia and the Pacific. New York: United Nations Publications,
annual.

Country-by-country statistics on agricultural and industrial production, etc.

Nonprint Resources

China: The Enduring Heritage. Indiana University Audio-Visual Center, Bloomington,
IN 47405.

A series of films on Chinese history through art, produced by the noted art
historian Wango Weng. 16mm.

"One Village in China"; "Small Happiness"; "First Moon." New Day Films, 22
Riverview Drive, Wayne, NJ 07470.

Tradition and modernity in the North China village of Long Bow. 16 mm. or
VHS.

"Zengbu After Mao." Center for Visual Anthropology, University of Southern California, Los Angeles, CA 90089.

Portrait of changes in a village in Guangzhou Province. VHS.

"Looking at China/Looking at America." China Council of The Asia Society, 725
Park Avenue, New York, NY 10021.

How Chinese and Americans have perceived, and misperceived, each other
throughout two centuries. Slide/audio tape set.

The Dragon and the Eagle: The American Experience in China. James Culp Productions, Image House West, 1259A Folsom Street, San Francisco, CA 94103.

> Set of five films describing the American experience in China during the twentieth century, using rare archival footage. 16 mm. or VHS.

Department of Performances, Films, and Lectures, The Asia Society, 725 Park Avenue, New York, NY 10021.

> A good source of information about films and videotapes on China. Videotapes of performances of Chinese music and dance are available for rental from the same source.

Embassy of the People's Republic of China, 2300 Connecticut Avenue N.W., Washington, DC 20008.

> Various documentary films on China are available through the embassy.

Coordination Council for North American Affairs, 4201 Wisconsin Avenue N.W., Washington, DC 20016.

> Various documentary films on Taiwan are available through the Republic of China's "unofficial embassy" in Washington.

Feature Films

The Good Earth (USA, 1937)

> A film version of Pearl Buck's Pulizer Prize-winning novel: Horatio Alger-style success story in Chinese clothing.

Princess Yang Kuei-fei (Japan, 1957)

> Kenji Mizoguchi's lovely cinematic retelling of Bo Juyi's Tang poem "The Song of Unending Regret."

The Great Wall Is a Great Wall (USA, 1985)

> Director Peter Wang also stars in this comedy about a Chinese American who goes back to China to visit his family.

Nixon in China (USA, 1987)

> Videotape of the Houston Opera Company production of this contemporary opera by John Adams and Alice Goodman.

The Last Emperor (USA, 1987)

> Bertolucci's Oscar-winning extravaganza.

Red Detachment of Women (China, 1960s)

    Film version of the famous "model revolutionary ballet" of the Cultural Revolution era.

Xu Mao and His Daughters; *In the Wild Mountains*; *The Black Cannon Incident* (China, 1980s)

    These three films are typical of the best works of Chinese cinema in the post-Mao era.

A Summer at Grandpa's; *Dust in the Wind* (Taiwan, 1980s)

    Autobiographical films by young director Hou Hsiao-hsien, typical of Taiwan's "new cinema" of the 1980s.

Suggestions for
Further Reading

(Chapter I)

Kwang-chih Chang, ed. *Food in Chinese Culture.* New Haven: Yale University Press, 1977.

Essays on the cultural importance of food throughout Chinese history.

Richard W. Wilson. *Learning to be Chinese.* Cambridge: M.I.T. Press, 1970.

A study of how young children in Taiwan learn Chinese political values.

Frank Ching. *Ancestors.* New York: William Morrow, 1988.

A Chinese *Roots*—900 years of Chinese history seen through the story of the author's forebears.

Maxine Hong Kingston. *The Woman Warrior.* New York: Alfred A. Knopf, 1977.

Memoirs of a young Chinese-American woman; a fascinating reflection on what it means to be Chinese.

(Chapter II)

J. E. Spencer and William L. Thomas. *Asia East by South: A Cultural Geography.* New York: John Wiley & Sons, 1971.

    An excellent treatment of the geographic context of Asian culture.

Owen Lattimore. *Inner Asian Frontiers of China.* New York: American Geographical Society, 1940.

    A classic study of cultural interactions along China's borders.

Journey Into China. Washington: National Geographic Society, 1976.

    A beautifully illustrated survey of China's various regions.

(Chapter III)

Ch'ao-Ting Chi. *Key Economic Areas in Chinese History.* London: George Allen & Unwin, 1936.

    The standard work on China's economic history, with emphasis on water-control projects.

Wolfgang Bauer. *China and the Search for Happiness: Recurring Themes in Four Thousand Years of Chinese Cultural History.* New York: The Seabury Press, 1976.

    Perspectives on Chinese social ideals. Difficult reading, but full of insights.

Etienne Balazs. *Chinese Civilization and Bureaucracy.* New Haven: Yale University Press, 1964.

    Collected essays of one of the world's foremost students of Chinese social history.

(Chapter IV)

Kwang-chih Chang. *The Archaeology of Ancient China*, 4th ed. New Haven: Yale University Press, 1987.

    The standard work in the field; comprehensive but somewhat technical.

Herlee Glessner Creel. *The Birth of China.* New York: Frederick Ungar Publishing Co., 1937.

    Now out of date on some details, but still the best popular introduction to ancient China.

Michael Loewe. *Everyday Life in Early Imperial China.* New York: G. P. Putnam's Sons, 1968.

An accurate and very readable account of life during the Han Dynasty.

Arthur F. Wright and Denis Twitchett, eds. *Perspectives on the T'ang.* New Haven: Yale University Press, 1973.

A collection of essays by various scholars that give a good picture of Tang society.

(Chapter V)

Jacques Gernet. *Daily Life in China on the Eve of the Mongol Invasion, 1250–1276.* New York: The Macmillan Company, 1962.

A brilliant evocation of life in the Southern Song capital at Hangzhou.

Morris Rossabi. *Khubilai Khan: His Life and Times.* Berkeley: University of California Press, 1988.

A sympathetic account of the Yuan Dynasty's greatest emperor.

Charles O. Hucker. *The Traditional Chinese State in Ming Times (1368–1644).* Tucson: University of Arizona Press, 1961.

A brief and clear account of the organization and functions of government during the Ming Dynasty.

Susan Naquin and Evelyn S. Rawski. *Chinese Society in the Eighteenth Century.* New Haven: Yale University Press, 1987.

A comprehensive portrait of Chinese society at the height of the late imperial era.

(Chapter VI)

P'ing-ti Ho. *The Ladder of Success in Imperial China: Aspects of Social Mobility, 1368–1911.* New York: Columbia University Press, 1962.

A classic study of the civil service examinations and social mobility in late imperial China.

Hsiao-t'ung Fei. *China's Gentry.* Chicago: University of Chicago Press, 1968.

Essays on aspects of upper-class life in late imperial China, by China's greatest modern social historian.

Ida Pruitt. *A Daughter of Han: The Autobiography of a Chinese Working Woman.* Stanford: Stanford University Press, 1967.

The society of late traditional China as seen by an ordinary working woman who told her story to an American social worker in the 1930s.

Derk Bodde and Clarence Morris. *Law in Imperial China.* Cambridge: Harvard University Press, 1967.

Translations of records of 190 Qing Dynasty court cases, with an excellent
introductory essay on the role of law in traditional Chinese society.

The Judge Dee mystery novels of Robert H. Van Gulik (*Celebrated Cases of Judge Dee*;
The Chinese Gold Murders; others in the same series: various publishers and dates)
Written in authentic Chinese style by a famous China scholar. They give an
excellent picture of Chinese government and society in the Ming period.

(Chapter VII)

Arthur Waley. *Three Ways of Thought in Ancient China*. New York: The Macmillan
Company, 1939.

A brief, readable introduction to Daoism, Confucianism, and Legalism in the
Zhou period, seen through the writings of Zhuangzi, Mencius, and Han Feizi.

Yu-lan Fung. *A Short History of Chinese Philosophy*. New York: The Macmillan
Company, 1948.

A standard work on Chinese philosophy from earliest times to the twentieth
century.

Laurence G. Thomson. *Chinese Religion: An Introduction*, 4th ed. Belmont, CA:
Wadsworth, 1988.

The best brief study of the whole spectrum of religion in China.

Wei-ming Tu. *Confucian Thought: Selfhood as Creative Transformation*. Ithaca, NY:
State University of New York Press, 1987.

Essays on the personal and religious dimensions of Confucianism, by a contemporary Confucian philosopher.

Michael Loewe. *Chinese Ideas of Life and Death*. London: George Allen & Unwin,
1982.

Discusses the Han Dynasty foundations of the main themes in Chinese religion.

(Chapter VIII)

Robert K. G. Temple. *China: Land of Discovery and Invention*. Wellingborough,
England: Patrick Stephens, 1986.

A well-illustrated popular condensation of Joseph Needham's massive *Science
and Civilisation in China*.

Sung Ying-hsing. *T'ien-Kung K'ai-Wu: Chinese Technology in the Seventeenth Century*.

E-tu Zen Sun and Shiou-chuan Sun, tr. University Park: Pennsylvania State University Press, 1966.

A translation, nicely illustrated with woodblock prints, of a Chinese encyclopedia of technology written in 1637.

Rudolf P. Hommel. *China at Work.* New York: The John Day Company, 1937. (Reprinted, Cambridge: M.I.T. Press, 1969).

A description, with excellent photographs, of traditional technology still in use in China in the early twentieth century.

Nathan Sivin. *Traditional Medicine in Contemporary China.* Ann Arbor: University of Michigan Center for Chinese Studies, 1988.

An account of both the theory and practice of traditional Chinese medicine; one of the few reliable works in this field.

(Chapter IX)

Michael Sullivan. *The Arts of China*, 3rd ed. Berkeley: University of California Press, 1984.

The best single-volume survey of Chinese art, ancient to modern.

Maggie Keswick. *The Chinese Garden.* London: Academy Editions, 1978.

Discusses the garden in relation to art, architecture, and cultural history.

Burton Watson. *Early Chinese Literature.* New York: Columbia University Press, 1962.

A good introduction to classical literature from earliest times to the Han Dynasty.

Edward H. Schafer. *The Golden Peaches of Samarkand.* Berkeley: University of California Press, 1963.

One of several books by this author that explore the poetic imagery of the Tang Dynasty.

Cyril Birch, ed. *Anthology of Chinese Literature.* New York: Evergreen Books, 1965.

Wide ranging and well selected, this anthology includes works of poetry, prose, and drama.

Harold R. Isaacs, ed. *Straw Sandals: Chinese Short Stories, 1918–1933.* Cambridge: M.I.T. Press, 1974.

A good, representative collection of stories in the new vernacular prose of the May Fourth Movement.

(Chapter X)

John K. Fairbank. *The Great Chinese Revolution, 1800–1985.* New York: Harper & Row, 1987.

> A masterful survey of the fall of traditional China and the various stages of the Chinese revolution.

Frederic Wakeman Jr. *Strangers at the Gate: Social Disorder in South China, 1839–1861.* Berkeley: University of California Press, 1966.

> Brilliant analysis of the impact—direct and indirect—of the Opium War in South China.

Mary C. Wright. *The Last Stand of Chinese Conservatism.* Stanford: Stanford University Press, 1957.

> The self-strengthening movement, and why it failed.

Lucien Bianco. *The Origins of the Chinese Revolution, 1915–1949.* Stanford: Stanford University Press, 1971.

> Particularly good on the May Fourth Movement and the role of ideas in the Chinese revolution.

(Chapter XI)

Maurice Meisner. *Mao's China and After.* Stanford: Stanford University Press, 1986.

> An excellent interpretive history of China since 1949.

Chen Jo-hsi. *The Execution of Mayor Yin and Other Stories from The Great Proletarian Cultural Revolution.* Bloomington: Indiana University Press, 1978.

> Vivid portrayals, in fiction, of the "ten terrible years," 1966–1976.

Harry Harding. *China's Second Revolution: Reform After Mao.* New York: The Council on Foreign Relations, 1987.

> The best comprehensive analysis of the reform policies of Deng Xiaoping.

Thomas B. Gold. *State and Society in the Taiwan Miracle.* Armonk, NY: M. E. Sharpe & Co., 1986.

> A balanced account of Taiwan's alternative path to modernization, by one of America's leading experts on Taiwan.

Frank Ching. *Hong Kong and China: For Better or For Worse.* New York: The Foreign Policy Association/The Asia Society, 1985.

> An analysis of the Sino-British agreement on Hong Kong's return to Chinese sovereignty in 1997.

(Chapter XII)

Alasdair Clayre. *The Heart of the Dragon.* New York: Houghton Mifflin, 1985.

This companion volume to the acclaimed PBS television series gives a vivid sense of the texture of ordinary Chinese life.

Ronald G. Knapp. *China's Traditional Rural Architecture: The Cultural Geography of the Common House.* Honolulu: University of Hawaii Press, 1986.

Beautifully illustrated, this volume shows how ordinary people live all over China.

Emily Honig & Gail Hershatter. *Personal Voices: Chinese Women in the 1980s.* Stanford: Stanford University Press, 1987.

Shows how both tradition and modernization affect the lives of women in China today.

Zhang Xinxin and Sang Ye. *Chinese Lives: An Oral History of Contemporary China.* New York: Pantheon Books, 1987.

Brief biographies of Chinese people from all walks of life, based on interviews conducted by two Chinese journalists.

Mark Salzman. *Iron and Silk.* New York: Random House, 1986.

Experiences of a young American teaching English and studying martial arts in China.

(Chapter XIII)

China Briefing. Boulder, CO: Westview Press, annual.

An annual update on Chinese affairs, prepared by the China Council of The Asia Society.

Denis Fred Simon and Merle Goldman, eds. *Science and Technology in Post-Mao China.* Cambridge: Harvard Contemporary China Series, No. 5, 1988.

An analysis of China's scientific modernization, and of the role of science and technology in China's future.

Index

Numbers in *italics* refer to illustrations.